1,000
FACTS ABOUT
DINOSAURS,
FOSSILS, AND PREHISTORIC LIFE

PATRICIA DANIELS   FOREWORD BY DR. MATTHEW VRAZO

NATIONAL
GEOGRAPHIC
KiDS

WASHINGTON, D.C.

Dromaeosaurs and ducklike *Vegavis iaai*

TABLE OF CONTENTS

Triangular spikes grew from *Tarchia*'s enormous skull.

From as far back as I can remember, I always wanted to be a paleontologist. While other kids were playing with toys and video games, I was outside collecting animal bones and rocks, and wondering what fossils might be buried in the local mountains near my home in Philadelphia, Pennsylvania, U.S.A. One of my most cherished childhood books was a dinosaur encyclopedia, and I dreamed about one day discovering a dinosaur bone. Now that I am older, instead of dinosaurs, I mainly study invertebrate fossils, and specifically arthropods such as sea scorpions and crabs. But I still have that same sense of curiosity and wonder about the natural world.

Whether you are a fan of fearsome carnivorous dinosaurs or the most alien-looking arthropods, this is an incredibly exciting time to be a paleontologist. In recent years, paleontologists have figured out how quickly *Tyrannosaurus rex* moved, identified the color of dinosaur feathers, and discovered the oldest animal trace fossils—that is, the tracks made by early life. And it seems like every few weeks paleontologists are finding older and older examples of preserved soft tissues, including mummified dinosaur guts, 520-million-year-old arthropod brains, and a cluster of eggs being protected by a trilobite parent.

Of course, with every new discovery comes just as many new questions. Why are only some organisms preserved as fossils? What caused certain animals to go extinct at different times? What was the largest ever dinosaur? *1,000 Facts About Dinosaurs, Fossils, and Prehistoric Life* answers these and many other questions about all aspects of prehistoric life, from the smallest microorganism to the largest dinosaur.

What's more, this book includes facts on the many professional and amateur paleontologists who have made fossil finding and paleontology their life's work. I hope this book inspires you to look at the world around you a little more closely, and perhaps even start your own journey into paleontology. You never know: The next new fossil discovery may be hiding out in your own backyard!

Matthew Vrazo, Ph.D.
Research Associate, Department of Paleobiology,
Smithsonian National Museum of Natural History

Eurypterid, also known as a sea scorpion

10 FAST FACTS ABOUT

1 **LIFE ON EARTH BEGAN** IN THE OCEANS AT LEAST **3.5 BILLION YEARS AGO.**

2 **FOSSILS ARE THE PRESERVED REMAINS OR TRACES** of plants or animals that lived in prehistoric times.

3 Fossils tell us how life developed on **EARTH.**

4 IN THE LONG SPAN OF PREHISTORIC TIME, **LANDMASSES MOVED AROUND ON EARTH,** REGULARLY JOINING TOGETHER AND SPLITTING APART.

Eurasia

North America

Thetys

South America

Africa

India

Antarctica

Australia

Phanthalassa

5 AROUND 400 MILLION YEARS AGO, THE **FIRST FOUR-LEGGED ANIMALS** CAME OUT OF THE OCEANS TO LIVE ON LAND.

DINOSAURS, FOSSILS, AND PREHISTORIC LIFE

6 The **FIRST MAMMALS** appeared during the dinosaur years. After the dinosaurs became extinct, mammals evolved into many different shapes, and some grew very large.

7 More than **99 PERCENT OF ALL SPECIES** that ever lived **ARE NOW EXTINCT.**

8 **PALEONTOLOGY IS THE STUDY OF ANCIENT LIFE** from fossil remains.

9 Fossils preserve only a small fraction of ancient life. For every new creature we find, **THOUSANDS OF SPECIES HAVE VANISHED,** leaving nothing behind.

10 **DINOSAURS WALKED ON EARTH** for about 174 million years, from about 240 million years ago to 66 million years ago.

GEOLOGIC TIME

When scientists talk about prehistoric life, they use terms from the geologic timescale. This scale is a way of measuring the history of Earth and its life from the planet's formation about 4.55 billion years ago.

The biggest division in the geologic timescale is the eon. Eons are divided into eras, which are divided into periods. Periods can be further split into epochs and ages. When we talk about

prehistoric life and the fossils formed from it, most of the time we refer to periods, as in the timeline below.

The very earliest life, single-celled organisms, formed in the Precambrian time. Complex life, like trilobites, really took off about 485 million years ago (MYA) during the Cambrian period in what is called the Cambrian explosion.

Dimetrodon

Graptolites

Stethacanthus

PERIOD	CAMBRIAN	ORDOVICIAN	SILURIAN	DEVONIAN	CARBONIFEROUS	PERMIAN	
WHEN	541–485 million years ago (MYA)	485–444 MYA	444–419 MYA	419–359 MYA	359–299 MYA	299–252 MYA	
NEW LIFE	hard-bodied sea creatures	first fish	millipedes on land	first sharks, insects	amphibians	reptiles, flying insects	

Trilobite

Dendrerpeton

Chilopeda

Even though trilobites seem like creatures from the dawn of time, in geologic time they were practically born yesterday. Life is recent, and humans are among the most recent of all creatures.

Think of it this way: Imagine you are taking a one-hour walk through the history of Earth (somehow untouched by volcanic eruptions and rising seas). For almost the entire walk—52 minutes—you would see nothing but barren rock and oceans—no life that could become a fossil.

Toward the end of that 52 minutes, if you scooped up some seawater, you might spot a few jellyfish, worms, sponges, or even shellfish like clams.

Your walk is almost over, but in the next four minutes, things get busy. Fish splash in the ocean, ferns grow on land, and amphibians and reptiles walk beside you. In the last four minutes, dinosaurs appear and disappear, surrounded by birds, flowers, and the first mammals. A few of these will become future fossils.

When do you see humans? Only as you take your last step across the finish line, right before you hit 60 minutes.

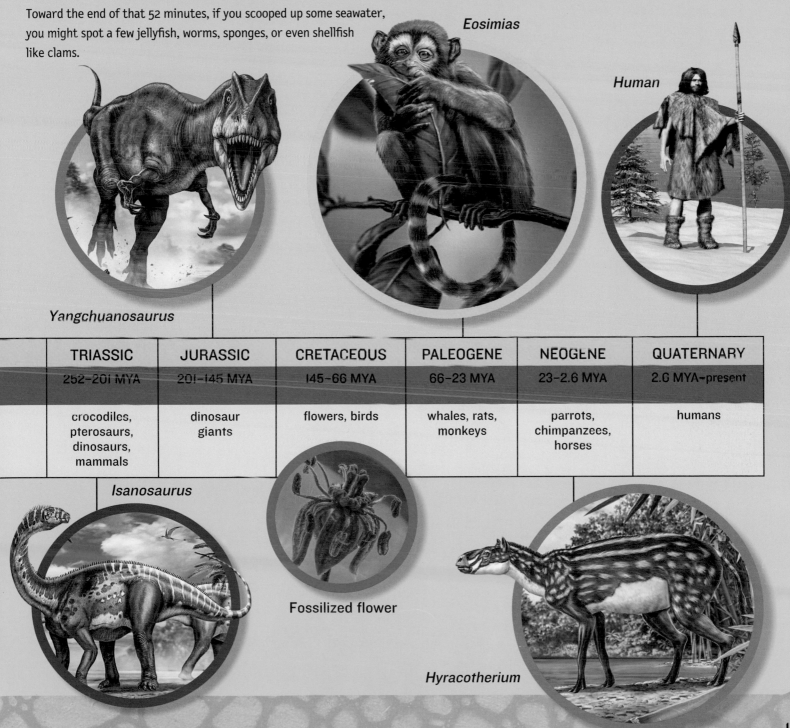

Eosimias

Human

Yangchuanosaurus

TRIASSIC	JURASSIC	CRETACEOUS	PALEOGENE	NEOGENE	QUATERNARY
252–201 MYA	201–145 MYA	145–66 MYA	66–23 MYA	23–2.6 MYA	2.6 MYA–present
crocodiles, pterosaurs, dinosaurs, mammals	dinosaur giants	flowers, birds	whales, rats, monkeys	parrots, chimpanzees, horses	humans

Isanosaurus

Fossilized flower

Hyracotherium

FOSSIL SITES

Fossils of dinosaurs and other prehistoric life can be found all over the world, but some places are known as fossil treasure troves.

Sites that have especially well-preserved fossils are known to paleontologists as *Lagerstätten* (LAH-geh-shteh-ten). This German word means "storage places." Locations such as Solnhofen, in Germany, the Burgess shale in western Canada, or the Yixian formation in eastern China are famous for their fantastic fossils. Argentina has giant dinosaurs, the La Brea Tar Pits in California, U.S.A., hold mammals, and Kenya is known for remarkable early remains of hominids—members of the human family.

Many of these places are deserts or rock quarries now, but in ancient times, climates were different and continents were snuggled together, far from where they are today. Oceans covered lands that are now dry; warm swamps dotted places that are currently frozen. What these sites have in common is that the animals or plants there suffered a sudden death and were preserved quickly. Floods or landslides might have buried them in mud that kept their bodies from decaying. Over time, the mud turned to rock, trapping the fossils in place.

This map shows some famous fossil sites. Some have been found only in recent years. Surely more will be discovered in the years to come.

NORTH AMERICA

Burgess Shale, British Columbia
Cambrian creatures such as *Hallucigenia*

Hell Creek, Montana
T. rex specimens and other late Cretaceous dinosaurs

Utah
Cambrian trilobites, Jurassic dinosaurs

Mazon Creek Beds, Illinois
Carboniferous creatures, including insects, fish, and amphibians

La Brea Tar Pits, California
Pleistocene mammals such as mammoths and saber-toothed cats

SOUTH AMERICA

Crato Formation, Brazil
Cretaceous pterosaurs, fish

Ischigualasto, Argentina
Triassic dinosaurs such as *Eoraptor*

Plaza Huincul, Argentina
Giant Cretaceous dinosaurs such as *Giganotosaurus*

• Dinosaur fossil location

AROUND THE WORLD

Rhynie, Scotland
Devonian plants and arthropods

Orsten, Sweden
Cambrian arthropods, soft organisms

EUROPE

Solnhofen, Germany
Jurassic species including *Archaeopteryx*, pterosaurs, and marine reptiles

Siberia, Russia
Cenozoic woolly mammoths

The Gobi, Mongolia
Cretaceous dinosaurs, eggs

ASIA

Yixian Formation, Liaoning, China
Cretaceous dinosaurs, birds

Guizhou Province, China
Precambrian and Cambrian microorganisms, trilobites

The Sahara, Niger
Cretaceous dinosaurs

AFRICA

Lake Turkana, Kenya
Cenozoic hominids

Madagascar
Cretaceous dinosaurs, reptiles, birds, mammals

Gogo Formation, West Australia
Devonian fish, arthropods

Lark Quarry, Queensland
Cretaceous dinosaur tracks

AUSTRALIA

Riversleigh, Queensland
Cenozoic mammals, birds, reptiles

Soom Shale, South Africa
Ordovician trilobites, arthropods, soft organisms

Ediacara Hills, South Australia
Precambrian organisms

75 ANCIENT FACTS ABOUT FOSSILS

❶ Paleontologists have found about 250,000 species of fossil animals and plants.

❷ Preserved remains can be called fossils if they are at least 10,000 years old.

❸ Hard things that turn into fossils, such as shells, bones, or wood, are called body fossils.

❹ Ancient footprints, nests, and burrows can turn into trace fossils. They show us how prehistoric animals lived and moved.

❺ Mold fossils hold the shape of a plant or animal that has rotted away, leaving an imprint in stone.

❻ Most fossils are found in sedimentary rock, which is made from sand, mud, and remains of plants and animals that are pressed together.

❼ Many fossils have been discovered by amateur fossil hunters, including kids!

❽ The most commonly found fossils come from hard-shelled underwater creatures such as clams or ammonites.

❾ OLDER FOSSILS ARE FOUND IN OLDER ROCKS. YOUNGER FOSSILS ARE FOUND IN YOUNGER ROCKS, WHICH ARE LAYERED ON TOP OF THE OLDER ROCKS.

❿ Sometimes rock layers are bent or twisted over time, moving fossils around.

⓫ It's easier to find fossils in exposed rocky places, such as deserts, where searchers can see them sticking out of the ground.

⓬ Some geologic ages are named for the place where their fossils and rocks were first studied. The Jurassic period is named after Europe's Jura Mountains.

⓭ Fossils are more common in limestone, which has lots of shells, and in shale, which has impressions formed from mud.

⓮ INDEX FOSSILS ARE FOSSILS THAT BELONG TO ONE SPECIFIC TIME PERIOD.

⓯ Ammonites are classic index fossils. Each species of ammonite can be linked to a particular time period.

⓰ Most fossils aren't found whole because their soft tissue rotted away.

⓱ Microfossils are the remains of tiny organisms. You need a microscope to see them well.

⓲ A subfossil is a bone or organism that is less than 10,000 years old and only partly fossilized.

⓳ Fossils can be dated by measuring the radioactive elements in the rocks that hold them. These elements decay at a steady rate, telling us how old the rocks are.

⓴ Fossils themselves can be radioactive if they have absorbed radioactive elements.

㉑ Most fossils come from plants or animals that died in or near water.

㉒ Fossils usually form when an organism is quickly buried by sediments, such as sand or mud, that stop it from rotting away.

㉓ Over time, sediments around the organism harden into sedimentary rock.

㉔ When mineral-rich water seeps into remains, the organism may slowly turn into rock in the exact shape of the original creature.

㉕ TRACE FOSSILS FORM WHEN FOOTPRINTS OR BURROWS ARE QUICKLY FILLED BY SEDIMENT, WHICH HARDENS INTO ROCK.

㉖ An organism can begin to harden a few weeks after it dies, but it can take hundreds or millions of years to turn into a fossil. The time depends on how big the organism is and what kind of minerals are in its surroundings.

㉗ The mile-deep cliffs of the Grand Canyon have fossils ranging from one billion to 270 million years old—but no dinosaurs.

㉘ ON AVERAGE, SCIENTISTS DISCOVER THE FOSSILS OF ONE NEW DINOSAUR SPECIES EACH WEEK.

㉙ Fossils from some parts of the world, such as Africa and Asia, have not been studied as much as those in other places, such as North America or Europe.

㉚ Transitional fossils show an organism partway through its evolution to its modern shape.

㉛ Complete fossils of soft-bodied animals are rare and treasured.

㉜ Scars and holes in fossil bones can tell us about ancient animals' veins and muscles.

Plant fossil dating from the Triassic period

33 Because they're found worldwide, fossils such as the fern *Glossopteris* show us how continents have moved over the ages.

34 Fossils also tell us how Earth's climate has changed from hot to cold and back again.

35 SOME FOSSIL ANIMALS ARE FLATTENED OUT. PALEONTOLOGISTS CALL THEM "ROADKILL."

36 Fossil bones aren't always found where the animal died. Bones are carried to new places by water or scavengers.

37 Trace fossils, such as footprints, are rarely found next to the creature that made them.

38 Long-living species are more likely to appear in the fossil record than those that became extinct quickly.

39 Some trace fossils show where an animal lay down for a nap.

40 Animals and plants that lived in the mountains rarely fossilize. Their bodies erode too quickly.

41 Organisms in wet jungles decay rapidly when they die and usually don't become fossils.

42 The ancient Greek scholar Xenophanes correctly pointed out that fossils of sea creatures found on dry land showed that some parts of the dry world were once underwater.

43 After studying fossils in the 1700s, French naturalist Georges Cuvier suggested that some animal species had become extinct.

44 Eleventh-century Persian scientist Ibn Sina correctly guessed that fossil plants and animals had been hardened by minerals from within the earth.

45 Ancient Greek writer Phlegon of Tralles wrote that huge animal fossils in North Africa proved that life was getting smaller over time. Later, Edward Drinker Cope's rule stated the opposite!

46 Fossils are often discovered when movements like earthquakes, erosion, or human construction bring them to the surface.

47 The pressure of the surrounding rock can sometimes smush a fossil into just a flat film, or imprint, made of carbon.

48 Some fossil animals and plants are trapped in amber, a sticky tree sap that hardens into a clear golden solid frame.

49 In some places, tar—a thick, sticky liquid—seeps up from the ground to trap and preserve unwary animals.

50 THE WORLD'S COLDEST PLACES, SUCH AS RUSSIA'S SIBERIA, ARE NATURAL FREEZERS, PRESERVING ANIMALS SUCH AS MAMMOTHS IN ICY SOIL.

51 Fossils can be natural mummies! In very dry parts of the world, dried-out animal bodies and parts—including dinosaur skins—can last for thousands of years.

52 Coal is a "fossil fuel." Ancient swamp plants were buried, squished, and heated, until they became black, shiny chunks we use for fuel.

53 Petroleum, or crude oil, is also a fossil fuel. It comes from early sea plants and micro-organisms that were buried, compressed, and mixed with sediments deep in the ground.

54 Trace fossils are also called ichnofossils. *Ichno* is the Greek word for "trace."

55 Eggs and nests can turn into fossils. They are important clues to dinosaur family life.

56 Side-to-side fossil scratches can mark where an animal was grazing for food.

57 EVEN SPIDER TRACKS CAN BECOME DELICATE TRACE FOSSILS.

58 The oldest trace fossils date back about 1.8 billion years and are trails probably made by single-celled organisms.

59 Coprolites—fossilized poop—can help a paleontologist because they may hold bits of an animal's last meal.

60 Ancient shark coprolites have a special spiral shape.

61 Soft-bodied worms don't fossilize, but their burrows harden in sediment.

62 Mysterious fossil trails found in Wisconsin, U.S.A., look like motorcycle tracks. They may have come from a huge, sluglike Cambrian creature.

63 *Asteriacites* are starlike impressions where ancient sea stars dug into the seafloor.

64 Bite traces on fossil bones tell us how animals were attacked—and sometimes what attacked them.

65 Germany's Solnhofen limestone preserved the curving track of the horseshoe crab *Mesolimulus*, and the crab itself. It is rare to find an animal with its tracks.

66 Dinosaur tracks found in Massachusetts, U.S.A., in 1802 were said by a collector to be from the biblical Noah's raven.

67 The distances between fossil footprints tell scientists whether an animal was walking, trotting, or running.

68 Enormous footprints from Cretaceous sauropods, plant-eating dinosaurs, have been found in Australia and measure 5.5 feet (1.7 m) long—the size of an adult human.

69 Fossilized burrows and tunnels, called domichnia, are trace fossils that preserve an animal's ancient home.

70 Some trace fossils are tiny trails on either side of an animal's body, left by its legs.

71 Fossilized bones that are swollen or misshapen can tell us about an animal's diseases.

72 IN 2012, AN EMPLOYEE AT NASA'S GODDARD SPACE FLIGHT CENTER WAS EATING LUNCH NEAR THE CENTER'S PARKING LOT WHEN HE SPOTTED ONE OF THE BIGGEST GROUPS OF DINOSAUR AND MAMMAL TRACKS EVER FOUND—MORE THAN 100.

73 A 565-million-year-old pencil-size trail, preserved as a trace fossil at Canada's Mistaken Point, may be the earliest record on Earth of animal movement.

74 The tiny, spiny skeletons of sponges are common fossils, found all over the world.

75 Things that look like fossils but aren't are called pseudofossils.

15 FANCIFUL FACTS ABOUT

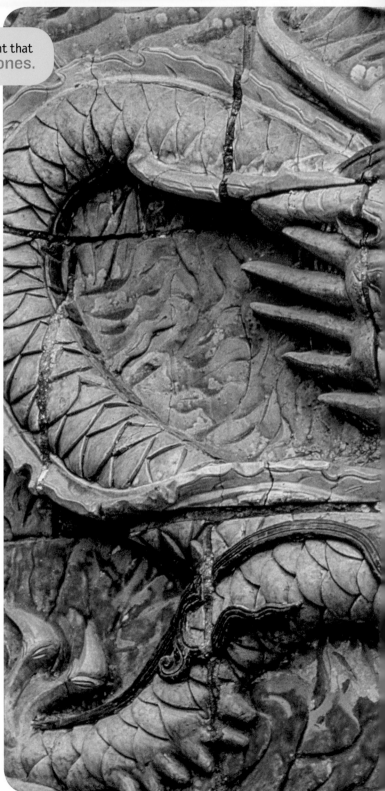

❶ In ancient China, people thought that dinosaur fossils were **dragon bones.**

❷ Ancient Greek historian **Herodotus** described fossils he saw in Egypt as "**the backbones and ribs of such serpents as it is impossible to describe.**"

❸ Ancient Roman naturalist **Pliny the Elder** wrote that "**tongue stones**" (actually fossilized shark teeth) fell from the sky during lunar eclipses.

❹ Medieval Europeans believed that the fossilized teeth of *Lepidotes, an ancient fish,* came from the head of a toad and could protect against poison.

❺ **Belemnites,** spearlike fossils from early squidlike animals, used to be called **thunderbolts** because people believed they were thrown to Earth during thunderstorms.

❻ A fifth-century Chinese scholar claimed that **brachiopod fossils flew about like birds** during thunderstorms.

❼ Fossil *Gryphaea* shells were once known as **devil's toenails** and could supposedly cure joint pain in people as well as in horses.

FOSSIL FOLKLORE

A dragon on the Nine-Dragon Wall in China's Forbidden City

8 Skulls of the dinosaur *Protoceratops* may have inspired legends of griffins, creatures with lion bodies and eagle wings.

9 A woolly rhinoceros fossil kept in a hall in Austria was said to come from a dragon called the **"Lindwurm."**

10 According to English folklore, anyone who kept a **fairy loaf—a fossil echinoid—**in their house would **never be without bread.**

11 In Swedish folktales, belemnite fossils **protected children from trolls.**

12 In 1726, German doctor Johann Beringer published descriptions of fossil crabs and **star-shaped patterns** he had found, only to discover that they had been carved and left for him as a practical joke. They are now known as **Beringer's Lying Stones.**

13 Some early naturalists thought that a "plastic force" from inside Earth made fossils such as sharks' teeth grow out of the stone around them.

14 The Greek myth of the one-eyed giant Cyclops may be based on fossil skulls of dwarf elephants, which have a single large hole.

15 *Protocardia,* rounded fossil shells, were once known as bulls' hearts in England.

❶ Stromatolites—columns of single-celled life-forms—lived in the oceans **3.5 billion years ago,** and still live on Earth today.

❷ The big swimming Cambrian predator *Anomalocaris* had a ring of sharp teeth and compound eyes like an insect.

❸ Geologist Reg Sprigg was eating lunch in the **Ediacara Hills of South Australia** when he discovered some of the **oldest fossils** known: blob-shaped, jellyfish-like imprints almost **600 million years old.**

❹ The earliest forms of life arose in the Precambrian time, before the Cambrian period began around 541 million years ago.

❺ Soft-bodied Ediacaran creatures had no heads, mouths, or guts.

❻ Many of the earliest **fossils are so mysterious-looking** that scientists aren't sure if they are animals or plants.

❼ The Cambrian animal *Wiwaxia* looked like a slug covered with scales and spines.

8 One of the most important Precambrian fossils, the **leaflike *Charnia,*** was discovered by a **15-year-old student** while he was rock climbing in England.

9 *Dickinsonia,* one of the largest Precambrian life-forms, looked like a round place mat. It was named for South Australian mines director Ben Dickinson. Paleontologists think it was an animal, but they're not sure.

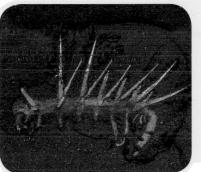

10 Paleontologists first thought the Cambrian creature *Hallucigenia* had spiny legs and tentacles on its back. Then they realized they had it upside down: The tentacles were its legs, and the spines grew from its back.

11 **Single-celled organisms** were the only form of life for most of Earth's history.

12 The sluglike *Kimberella,* found in Australia, likely scraped its food off the ocean floor.

13 The Burgess shale, in the Canadian Rockies, holds a wealth of 500-million-year-old Cambrian life-forms in amazing shapes.

14 The *Ottoia* worm, fossilized in Canada's Burgess shale, burrowed into the seafloor and grabbed prey with its snout.

15 Fossils from early Earth give us **clues to how life might develop** on other planets.

A fossil discovery at Ediacara Hills, in South Australia

THE CAMBRIAN
EXPLOSION

Fossil hunters studying rock layers more than 541 million years old will be lucky to find anything. At best, they might spot some tiny, jellyfish-like impressions in the stone. But if they lift their eyes just a few feet up to slightly younger rocks—what riches! Fossils of trilobites, mollusks, sponges, and many other complex life-forms suddenly appear. This great blooming of life in the Cambrian period is called the Cambrian explosion. The Cambrian period dates from about 541 to 485 million years ago. The ancestors of almost all plants and animals living today first showed up then. The Cambrian is when we begin to see animals with backbones, and with heads, tails, fins, and legs. Because predators hunted the seas, their prey developed tough outer shells to protect them from big, biting teeth. They also developed the ability to search for food in the mud and burrow into hiding places. The Cambrian had some strange-looking creatures that don't live on Earth anymore, such as *Hallucigenia*, a wormlike animal with tentacles for legs and spikes guarding its back. The Cambrian explosion happened quickly in geological terms, but once new life appeared, it took tens of millions of years for it to evolve. The tree of life, which had only a few twigs before the Cambrian period, over time branched out into a wide and wonderful megaplant.

Anomalocaris, an aquatic predator, hunts on the seafloor.

SCIENTISTS are still trying to FIGURE OUT WHY LIFE TOOK OFF in the Cambrian period. RISING LEVELS OF OXYGEN IN THE OCEANS MAY HAVE HELPED NEW LIFE TO DEVELOP. Genes that control how animals grow may have STARTED TO TAKE EFFECT. As some ANIMALS BECAME PREDATORS, the STRUGGLE TO SURVIVE MAY HAVE SPED UP THE EVOLUTION of new prey species.

DID YOU KNOW?

1
Sponges, primitive sea animals, are among the **oldest multicelled creatures** known. One sponge fossil found in China dates back 600 million years.

2
Sponges, corals, echinoderms (sea star-like animals), and **brachiopods** (clamlike creatures) covered the ocean floor in Paleozoic times.

3
Ancient corals and bryozoans, like those today, were tiny creatures that **clustered together in communities** on rocks or the seafloor.

4
Early **coral animals were rarely preserved,** but their outer skeletons fossilized well and tell scientists a lot about early oceans.

5
Graptolites were wormlike colonies of connected animals whose fossils **look like scribbles in rock.** In fact, their name means "written on rock."

6
Brachiopods, shelled animals that **looked a little like today's clams,** are among the most common fossils from the Paleozoic era.

7
Trilobites crawled, burrowed, and swam in the world's oceans for more than **250 million years.**

8
Trilobites were arthropods, **like today's crabs, spiders, and scorpions.**

9
Ammonites were related to today's octopuses and squid, but they lived inside coiled shells.

10
Ammonites first appeared about **240 million years ago.**

11
Eurypterids, also called sea scorpions, were **scary predators of Paleozoic oceans.** They were arthropods, related to today's scorpions and crabs.

12
Fossils of **eurypterids** were usually formed from their **shed exoskeletons** and not their inner bodies.

13
Fossil brain corals look like the **grooved surface of a human brain.** Brain corals still look like that today.

14
Tiny **bryozoans** are **known as moss animals,** because their fossils look like a bed of moss.

15
Sometimes minerals that seep into fossil coral turn it into a shiny, colorful stone called agatized coral. **Agatized coral is Florida's state** gemstone.

16
The **Permian-Triassic extinction,** 252 million years ago, killed off almost all corals and bryozoans.

17
Trilobite fossils are found on every continent, including Antarctica.

18
Conulariids are mysterious four-sided fossils that may have been **jellyfish shaped like ice-cream cones.**

19
Many **ammonite shells** grew in a perfect mathematical shape sometimes called the **marvelous spiral.**

20
A colorful gemstone called **ammolite** is made from fossilized ammonite shells.

50

Floating Facts About
EARLY SEA CREATURES

Biofluorescent, or glowing, brain coral

21 Trilobite fossils have been found near the peaks of the Himalayan mountains.

22 Trilobites evolved into more than 20,000 species.

23 The *Archimedes* bryozoan fossil forms a perfect corkscrew shape.

24 Trilobite means "three-lobed." Their exoskeletons, seen from the top, had three lengthwise divisions.

25 Some trilobite fossils have amazingly detailed compound eyes. Their eyes contained the mineral calcite, which fossilizes well.

26 A trilobite appears on the coat of arms of Dudley, England. Local people call it the "Dudley bug."

27 Trilobites are also found in the walls of England's Dudley Castle.

28 Sea stars and their echinoderm relatives appeared in the oceans more than 400 million years ago.

29 Trilobites are the state fossils of Pennsylvania, Wisconsin, and Ohio, U.S.A.

30 Nautiloids were shelled ocean animals similar to ammonites. They survived the great extinction about 65 million years ago, while ammonites did not.

31 Trilobites ranged from fingernail-size creatures to *Isotelus rex*, 28 inches (71 cm) long.

32 Echinoderms had five-sided bodies, a rare shape for an animal.

33 The inner chambers of an ammonite shell were filled with gas so the animal could float. The outermost chamber held the animal's body.

34 The trilobite *Erbenochile's* eyes stood straight up from its head like a dog's ears.

35 Sea lilies were animals called crinoids that resembled sea stars, but they were attached to the seafloor by a stalk.

36 The flowerlike heads of stemmed crinoids actually held the animal's guts.

37 Spiny trilobites like *Comura* could roll up in a ball, presenting a prickly defense against predators.

38 Most ammonite fossils have lost their outer shell and show just the spiral inside their chambers.

39 The eurypterid *Pterygotus* was a predator more than five feet (1.5 m) long.

40 *Pterygotus* had a paddle-like tail that helped it swim after prey, and sharp claws to spear it.

41 Some ammonites were more than four feet (1.2 m) wide.

42 Ammonites had sharp beaks that they used to snatch up their prey.

43 Bivalve and brachiopod fossils, from different animal groups, both have two shells. Bivalve shells match in size; brachiopod shells do not.

44 Crinoids could grow to more than 130 feet (40 m) long, longer than two tractor-trailer trucks end to end.

45 Crinoid fossils often have a snail-like platyceratid fossil attached to them. The creature may have survived by drilling into the crinoid and eating its organs—and its poop!

46 Fossil gastropod shells range from plain cone shapes to spirals tightly coiled like a Slinky.

47 A Bronze Age woman in England was buried surrounded by more than 100 echinoderm fossils.

48 Echinoderm fossils are known in folklore as shepherd's crowns, starstones, and crystal apples.

49 Sometimes all that's left of an ancient echinoderm is its circular jaw with five sharp teeth, a shape known as Aristotle's lantern.

50 The nautiloid *Orthoceras* grew more than 19 feet (5.8 m) long, with thick tentacles and a beaked mouth.

75 DUG-UP FACTS ABOUT FOSSIL HUNTERS

1 Renaissance artist and inventor Leonardo da Vinci collected fossil shells and understood that they had been ancient sea animals.

2 Vertebrate paleontologists study the fossils of animals with backbones, such as dinosaurs.

3 Spanish conquistador Hernando Cortés brought a huge mastodon bone from Mexico back to Spain in 1519.

4 In 1785, artist Charles Willson Peale, famous for his portrait of George Washington, established the first American museum to show a mounted fossil skeleton (a mastodon).

5 President Thomas Jefferson loved fossils and wrote scientific papers about them. The giant ground sloth *Megalonyx jeffersonii* is named after him.

6 On their expedition to the American West in the early 1800s, explorers Meriwether Lewis and William Clark found fossils including mastodons and dinosaur ribs.

7 Paleontology students study geology, biology, chemistry, statistics, and computer programming.

8 Invertebrate paleontologists study fossils of animals without backbones, such as trilobites.

9 FAMED BRITISH FOSSIL HUNTER MARY ANNING FOUND A REPTILE-LIKE ICHTHYOSAUR FOSSIL IN A CLIFF IN 1811, WHEN SHE WAS ONLY 12 YEARS OLD.

10 In 1823, Anning was the first to discover the full skeleton of a plesiosaur, a prehistoric swimming reptile.

Imprints of 500-million-year-old trilobites in stone

11 When geologist Gideon Mantell showed naturalists the first discovered *Iguanodon* teeth in the 1820s, they dismissed them as fish or rhinoceros teeth.

12 British naturalist Charles Darwin collected thousands of fossils on his voyages to South America. They helped him form his theory of evolution.

13 Darwin found a fossil in Patagonia that looked like a combination of a rhino, giraffe, camel, and elephant. It is now known as *Macrauchenia*, an ancestor of horses.

14 In 1853, British scientist and artist Benjamin Waterhouse Hawkins hosted a dinner party inside the full-size model of an *Iguanodon* that he had built.

15 PALEOICHNOLOGISTS SPECIALIZE IN TRACE FOSSILS, SUCH AS ANIMAL FOOTPRINTS.

16 The 19th-century American paleontologist Barnum Brown collected so many fossils as a child that they had to go into a separate building near his home.

17 On one fossil-hunting expedition to South America, Brown was shipwrecked, but floated safely to shore holding a barrel.

18 Brown was one of the first people to encase fossils in a plaster cast to keep them safe when they traveled.

19 Brown collected so many fossils that even today they haven't all been unpacked.

20 IN 1902, BARNUM BROWN DISCOVERED THE FIRST *TYRANNOSAURUS REX* (*T. REX*) IN HELL CREEK, IN MONTANA, U.S.A.

21 Because he discovered so many fossils, Brown was nicknamed "Mr. Bones."

22 Paleobotanists are paleontologists who study fossil plants.

23 Australian paleobotanist Isabel Cookson studied fossil plants to learn how plants evolved.

24 The house of 19th-century English geologist William Buckland was filled with fossils and live animals—even a jackal.

25 In 1824, Buckland published the first description of a dinosaur based on huge fossils he had collected. He called it *Megalosaurus*, or "great lizard."

26 Buckland collected fossilized dinosaur poop and called it coprolite. He even had a table-top inlaid with coprolites.

27 Edward Drinker Cope, a 19th-century American paleontologist, discovered more than 1,000 extinct species. He is best known, however, for his bitter feud with his rival paleontologist, Othniel Charles Marsh.

28 The 19th-century fights between Cope and Marsh are now known as the "Bone Wars."

29 Marsh was the first to describe *Triceratops* and *Stegosaurus*.

30 In 1870, Marsh pointed out that Cope, his enemy, had mistakenly put the head of a fossil *Elasmosaurus* on the animal's tail.

31 Cope was so embarrassed by his mistake on the *Elasmosaurus* fossil that he tried to buy all the copies of the journal in which he had described the animal.

32 Workers for rival paleontologists Cope and Marsh would blow up their fossil fields rather than let the other team dig there.

33 Marsh was one of the first to suggest that modern birds are related to dinosaurs.

34 Nineteenth-century British paleontologist Richard Owen invented the term "dinosauria" to describe the first dinosaur fossils. The name means "terrible reptiles."

35 A team led by American explorer Roy Chapman Andrews discovered the first *Velociraptor* in the Gobi, in Mongolia.

36 ROY CHAPMAN ANDREWS MAY HAVE PARTLY INSPIRED THE FILM CHARACTER INDIANA JONES.

37 In Montana, American paleontologist Jack Horner found the first evidence that dinosaurs cared for their young. The *Jurassic Park* character Alan Grant was partly based on him.

38 Chinese paleontologist Xu Xing, who studies feathered dinosaur fossils, has named more prehistoric species than any other modern scientist.

39 Micropaleontologists study microfossils that can be seen well only with a microscope.

40 Nine-year-old Jude Sparks was playing in New Mexico, U.S.A., when he tripped and landed next to a rare *Stegomastodon* tusk.

41 Paleontologists braved 125°F (52°C) heat to dig up new dinosaur fossils in Mongolia and the Sahara.

42 In 1983, British fossil hunter William Walker discovered fish-eating dinosaur *Baryonyx* when he spotted a huge fossil claw in a clay pit.

43 ARGENTINE FOSSIL HUNTER JOSÉ BONAPARTE HAD NO FORMAL TRAINING IN PALEONTOLOGY, BUT HE DISCOVERED IMPORTANT DINOSAUR FOSSILS, INCLUDING *ARGENTINOSAURUS*.

44 Paleoanthropologists study fossilized human remains.

45 In 1959, British paleoanthropologist Mary Leakey discovered the first fossil *Australopithecus* skull, a 1.75-million-year-old ancestor of humans.

46 In 1976, Leakey's team found amazing trace fossils in Tanzania: human footprints, about 3.5 million years old.

47 In Africa, paleontologist Nizar Ibrahim found dinosaur bones and tracks in ancient riverbeds in the desert.

48 The first skeleton of *Yangchuanosaurus*, a huge predatory dinosaur, was discovered in 1977 by a construction worker in China.

49 American paleontologist Jim Kirkland found a dinosaur fossil treasure trove in Utah after a tip from a rock shop cashier.

50 German paleontologist Tilly Edinger founded paleoneurology: the study of fossil brains.

51 WILLIAM PARKER FOULKE, A LAWYER, DISCOVERED THE FIRST NEARLY COMPLETE FOSSIL SKELETON, A *HADROSAURUS*, IN 1858.

52 In Illinois, U.S.A., in 1955, pipe fitter Francis Tully found a fossil in a scrap heap that would be known as the "Tully monster."

53 American geologist William Orcutt specialized in finding oil, but he was the first to recognize that bones from the La Brea Tar Pits, in California, U.S.A., were prehistoric.

54 Palynologists study fossilized plant pollen.

55 In 2009, American high-school student Kevin Terris found an almost complete *Parasaurolophus* fossil in Utah.

56 In South Africa, nine-year-old Matthew Berger discovered a new species of fossil hominin (a close relative of humans). It was later named *Australopithecus sediba*.

57 Paleoecologists study how fossil organisms interacted with their surroundings, to help us understand the climate and ecology of the prehistoric world.

58 American geologist Earl Douglass discovered the first *Apatosaurus* when he saw eight tailbones sticking out of the ground near Vernal, Utah, in 1909.

59 While her fossil hunting team fixed a flat tire on the last day of their South Dakota, U.S.A., expedition, Sue Hendrickson took a last look and found the big *T. rex* fossil now called Sue.

60 Seven-year-old Ruth Mason found a huge bed of dinosaur bones on her family's South Dakota ranch in 1990. The area is now known as the Ruth Mason Dinosaur Quarry.

61 A fossil jaw from the collection gathered by the 18th-century Russian princess Yekaterina Dashkova was from *Elasmotherium sibiricum*, a giant rhinoceros.

62 American paleontologist Samuel Williston discovered the first big dinosaur fossil, *Diplodocus*, in Colorado in 1877.

63 Taphonomists are paleontologists who study how organisms become preserved as fossils.

64 In 1909, 13-year-old Stuart Walcott and his parents were riding horses through Canada's Burgess Pass when they saw rocks dislodged by a snow slide, containing beautiful crustacean fossils. The area would become the famous Burgess shale.

65 IN 2004, A SEVEN-YEAR-OLD CHILEAN BOY, DIEGO SUAREZ, DISCOVERED THE FIRST FOSSIL OF A *T. REX*-LOOKING DINOSAUR, NOW NAMED *CHILESAURUS DIEGOSUAREZI*.

66 New Zealand fossil hunter Joan Wiffen taught herself paleontology. In 1975, she found the first dinosaur fossils ever discovered in her country.

67 Scientist Louis Purnell was a Tuskegee Airman in WWII before becoming an expert on fossil nautiloids and cephalopods for the Smithsonian Institution.

68 Yang Zhongjian, also called C. C. Yang, pioneered Chinese paleontology. In the 20th century, he discovered such dinosaurs as *Yunnanosaurus* and the feathered *Zhongjianosaurus yangi*, which is named for him.

69 Inspired by a toy dinosaur he pulled out of a cereal box as a child, Canadian Philip Currie became a paleontologist and an expert in feathered dinosaurs and bird evolution.

70 MICHAEL ARSENAULT, A NINE-YEAR-OLD CANADIAN BOY, SLIPPED ON SANDSTONE NEAR HIS COTTAGE AND LANDED BY THE BACKBONE OF A NEW PREHISTORIC REPTILE, *ERPETONYX ARSENAULTORUM*.

71 A physicist named Bill Shipp was walking around his land in Montana, U.S.A., when he discovered the fossil leg bones of a new species of horned dinosaur. Nicknamed "Judith," the species is officially named *Spiclypeus shipporum*.

72 Canadian fossil preparer Wendy Sloboda has found new species on several continents. One, the dinosaur *Wendiceratops*, is named for her.

73 In Canada, paleontologist Elizabeth Nicholls dug up and transported the biggest ichthyosaur fossil ever discovered. It was 75 feet (23 m) long. She named it *Shonisaurus sikanniensis*.

74 American Alexander Wetmore, an expert on fossil birds who became the head of the Smithsonian in 1945, was a tidy man who wore a tie even while studying birds in the rainforest.

75 American paleontologist Robert Bakker was one of the first scientists to say that dinosaurs could be fast-moving, warm-blooded, and feathered.

1 FISH WERE THE FIRST VERTEBRATES—animals with backbones.

2 Placoderms, such as *DUNKLEOSTEUS,* had heavy armored heads with sharp, toothlike jaws.

3 The jawless fish *CEPHALASPIS* HAD EYES RIGHT ON TOP OF ITS HEAD so it could look out for predators above it.

4 Some scars on PLACODERM FOSSILS come from placoderm jaws—showing that the ARMORED FISH ATTACKED EACH OTHER.

5 The earliest fish had no jaws or teeth, but they did have BONY HEAD SHIELDS.

25 BITING FACTS ABOUT

6 FISH FOSSILS ARE OFTEN BROKEN and incomplete because fish bones were so delicate.

7 A PLACODERM FOSSIL from Antarctica revealed that the armored fish had SILVERY BELLIES AND RED BACKS.

8 Some PLACODERM JAWS HAD HINGES that allowed the animal's jaws to swing open in a huge bite.

9 The FIRST JAWED FISH were the size of minnows.

10 Nicknamed the "TULLY MONSTER," the *Tullimonstrum gregarium* fossil found in Illinois, U.S.A., HAD EYEBALLS ON STALKS STICKING OUT OF ITS BACK. Scientists think it was some kind of fish, but they aren't sure.

11 The Tully monster is the STATE FOSSIL OF ILLINOIS.

12 Scientists in Brazil found the first FOSSILIZED HEART ever discovered, in a fish called *RHACOLEPIS BUCCALIS.*

13 *EUSTHENOPTERON,* a big fish found in thousands of Canadian fossils, had bones in its front and back fins that show the **EARLY EVOLUTION OF LAND-WALKING LIMBS.**

14 The sharp teeth of *HELICOPRION,* **A SHARKLIKE RATFISH,** were arranged in a coil in the animal's lower jaw. When *Helicoprion* closed its mouth, the teeth would have torn into prey like a circular saw.

15 Scientists studying *CARCHAROCLES MEGALODON* jaws believe it could bite with **IO TIMES** the force of a modern great white shark.

16 **FOSSIL BUTTE, MONTANA, U.S.A.,** has rare complete fossils of **CENOZOIC STINGRAYS,** including one with baby stingrays surrounding it.

17 An adult human can stand upright in the jaws of a fossil *CARCHAROCLES MEGALODON.*

ANCIENT SHARKS
AND OTHER FIERCE FISH

18 *TIKTAALIK ROSEAE,* found in the Canadian Arctic in 2004, had fins like a fish but a head like a crocodile. It shows how four-legged animals **EVOLVED FROM SEA CREATURES.**

19 *TIKTAALIK* **PROBABLY WALKED AROUND ON ITS FINS** in shallow water.

20 **THE STATE FOSSIL OF NORTH CAROLINA,** U.S.A., is the *CARCHAROCLES MEGALODON* tooth.

21 *XENACANTHUS* sharks had a bony spine sticking backward from their heads. It might have been **VENOMOUS,** like stingray spines.

22 A fossil from America's Green River formation shows a *DIPLOMYSTUS* fish swallowing a *KNIGHTIA* fish. It may have **CHOKED TO DEATH ON ITS PREY.**

23 The **DEVONIAN PERIOD** is known as **THE AGE OF FISHES** because so many fish fossils are found in its rocks.

24 Seven-inch (18-cm)-long fossil teeth suggest that the gigantic Cenozoic shark *CARCHAROCLES MEGALODON* was up to **59 FEET** (18 m) long.

25 **PEOPLE RARELY FIND COMPLETE SHARK OR SKATE FOSSILS,** because their skeletons are made of cartilage that doesn't fossilize well.

15 HIGH-STEPPING FACTS

1 All land vertebrates are known as **tetrapods**, from the Greek words for "**four legs.**" Over time, some tetrapods evolved into legless forms such as snakes.

2 Fossils show that legs for walking developed from **fishlike fins.**

3 Fossilized footprints along the shore of Valentia Island in Ireland are those of an ancient tetrapod that **lived 385 million years ago.**

4 Early amphibians could be huge. *Prionosuchus* was an alligatorlike creature about 29.5 feet (9 m) long.

5 Modern salamanders are small, but *Metoposaurus*, a salamander ancestor, was **as big as a small car.**

6 Long spines sticking out of the backbone of *Dimetrodon* held a kind of sail. It may have helped to cool the animal, or attract mates.

7 *Eryops megacephalus* (the name means "large-headed drawn-out face") had an **enormous mouth**, a fifth the length of its body, filled with backward-pointing teeth.

Deinosuchus, an alligator ancestor, lunges at *Albertosaurus*.

ABOUT THE FIRST WALKERS

8 Sail-backed *Dimetrodon* looked like a dinosaur, a relative of ancient reptiles, but it was in fact **a distant ancestor of the first mammals.**

9 The early nonjumping frog, ***Triadobatrachus,*** is known from only one fossil found in Madagascar.

10 Devonian *Ichthyostegas,* one of the **first four-legged vertebrates,** had a tail like a fish, but also stumpy legs that would have allowed it to drag itself across land.

11 The brains of early reptiles were bigger than those of their amphibian ancestors. This may mean they had better hunting skills than earlier animals.

12 Fossil *Dendrerpeton,* early tetrapods, have been found inside fossil tree stumps in Nova Scotia, Canada. These amphibians might have died while taking shelter from forest fires.

13 Fossils of *Hylonomus,* one of the earliest known reptiles, are also found inside **ancient Nova Scotia tree stump.**

14 *Megachirella wachtleri,* a small reptile fossil found in the Italian Alps, dates back 240 million years. **It may be the oldest lizard ever found.**

15 *Deinosuchus,* a Cretaceous crocodile, was an impressive reptile. Based on a fossil skull found in Texas, U.S.A., it could grow to at least 32 feet (9.8 m) long—almost as long as a school bus.

MASS EXTINCTIONS

Almost all the animals that ever lived on Earth have become extinct—their species no longer exist. This die-off usually happens slowly when a species cannot compete against a rival, or when it cannot adapt to changing surroundings. However, the fossil record tells us that at five times in Earth's history, at least half of all species have died in a relatively quick, widespread mass extinction.

Scientists don't know for sure what caused most of these extinctions. Something probably drastically changed the environment, so that the temperatures and the atmosphere across the planet no longer supported most life.

Mass extinctions killed off life on Earth, but they also opened up space for new species to develop and spread out. By studying fossils that appeared after each mass extinction, scientists know that life bounced back. Mass extinctions always mark the boundary between one geologic period and another. The five big mass extinctions were:

ORDOVICIAN-SILURIAN, 440 million years ago
Cause: Dramatic cooling and glaciation, among other things. Almost all life lived in the sea then, and more than 60 percent of all species died.

DEVONIAN, 365 million years ago
Cause: Unclear. Up to 70 percent of marine life died out.

PERMIAN-TRIASSIC, 252 million years ago
Cause: Sudden climate change likely due to an asteroid impact or volcanic eruptions. Known as the Great Dying, this was the largest mass extinction in history. More than 90 percent of all species died out.

TRIASSIC-JURASSIC, 201 million years ago
Cause: Unclear. More than 70 percent of all species died, including archosaurs and many large amphibians.

CRETACEOUS-PALEOGENE, 65 to 66 million years ago
Cause: Possibly climate change from an asteroid strike or volcanic eruptions. About 75 percent of all species died out, including all dinosaurs except for birds.

DID YOU KNOW?

The most famous MASS EXTINCTION is the one that KILLED OFF ALL NON-BIRD DINOSAURS about 65 million years ago. THE DEADLIEST EXTINCTION, CALLED THE PERMIAN-TRIASSIC, happened 252 million years ago and WIPED OUT MORE THAN 90 PERCENT OF ALL SPECIES.

Duck-billed dinosaurs flee as an asteroid strikes the Gulf of Mexico.

1 *LEPIDODENDRON*— "scale trees"—stood tall when the first dinosaurs appeared. They grew **MORE THAN 100 FEET** (30 m) high, with a crown of branches at the very top.

2 One theory suggests that some dinosaurs **EVOLVED LONG NECKS** to nibble on the top of tall trees such as the **ARAUCARIA** evergreens.

3 ROBERT FALCON SCOTT'S 1912 expedition to the South Pole collected fossils of *Glossopteris*, a seed-bearing tree.

4 **FOSSILIZED TREES** found in Antarctica tell us that the continent was once much warmer, with plants that could **SURVIVE MONTHS OF DARKNESS.**

5 *GLOSSOPTERIS* fossils, found from South America to Africa and Antarctica, are important **EVIDENCE THAT THE CONTINENTS WERE JOINED** together in the distant past.

25 GREEN FACTS ABOUT

6 **PINE CONES** are sometimes fossilized in perfect detail.

7 Palmlike cycad plants date back to the **MESOZOIC ERA** and still live on Earth today.

8 Fossils found along a highway in West Virginia, U.S.A., turned out to be the oldest examples of **SEED-BEARING PLANTS** known, the Devonian ferns *ELKINSIA POLYMORPHA*.

9 Many of the earliest land PLANTS LOOKED LIKE FERNS. Some were short, some as tall as trees.

10 ANGIOSPERMS— FLOWERING PLANTS—AND PLANT-EATING DINOSAURS EVOLVED AT THE SAME TIME. The angiosperms may have flourished because they could grow back quickly after being munched.

11 Some of the oldest plants, such as *COOKSONIA,* **HAD NO ROOTS OR LEAVES.**

12 **THICK STUMPS OF FOSSIL TREES** make up a **"FOSSIL FOREST"** in the Catskill Mountains of New York, U.S.A.

13 Tiny bits of grass have been found in COPROLITES (DINOSAUR POOP) dating back 70 million years.

14 PATTERNS OF BITE MARKS ON FOSSIL LEAVES tell scientists which insects lived among ancient plants.

15 PLANT FOSSILS are often found in ancient lake bottoms or peat swamps. THE LOW-OXYGEN WATER PRESERVED PLANTS that fell into it instead of rotting them away.

16

THE FIRST FLOWERING PLANTS, such as *MONTSECHIA*, a slender lake plant, may have evolved in the water about 130 million years ago.

17 TINY POLLEN GRAINS FOSSILIZE WELL. They tell paleontologists a lot about the plants and climate in the prehistoric environment.

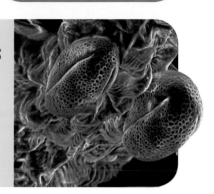

PREHISTORIC PLANTS

18 Like insects, prehistoric flowers are sometimes preserved in AMBER.

19 FOSSIL LEAVES trapped in ancient lake beds in Idaho, U.S.A., were so well preserved that they were still GREEN WHEN THE SURROUNDING ROCK was cracked open.

20 A beautiful, trumpet-shaped ASTERID FLOWER, found trapped in amber in the Dominican Republic, shows that flowering plants were growing in North America ABOUT 20 MILLION YEARS AGO.

21 Insect-eating plants go back to prehistoric times. Leaves from the Eocene carnivorous plant *RORIDULA* have been found in Russian amber mines.

22 Two-and-a-half-million-year-old PEACH PITS, looking just like the fruit pits of today, have been found in China. The PEACHES MIGHT HAVE BEEN SNACKS for early human ancestors.

23 WOOD TURNS INTO PETRIFIED WOOD— a fossil—when groundwater seeps in and replaces the wood tissue with minerals.

24

PETRIFIED WOOD can be extremely realistic, preserving tree rings and other details of the original tree.

25 Yellowstone National Park has its own PETRIFIED FOREST. Maples, oaks, dogwoods, and other trees became fossilized after they were BURIED BY VOLCANIC ASH 50 million years ago.

1 All ARTHROPODS—including trilobites, millipedes, and spiders—come from a COMMON ANCESTOR that lived at least 500 million years ago.

2 ARTHROPODS were probably common in prehistory, but in most species their THIN OUTER SKELETONS DIDN'T FOSSILIZE WELL.

3 AMBER starts as resin, a sticky goop that leaks out of cone-bearing trees. PREHISTORIC INSECTS could be TRAPPED IN IT before it hardened.

4 Creatures TRAPPED IN AMBER dry out quickly, so that tiny details such as HAIRS AND CELL STRUCTURE ARE PRESERVED.

5 Most FOSSIL ARACHNIDS are found preserved in amber or in fine-grained rock that kept DETAILED IMPRESSIONS of delicate animals.

6 A PIECE OF SPANISH AMBER, 110 MILLION YEARS OLD, holds strands from a spider's web with a mite, fly, wasp leg, and beetle trapped in the web.

7 The largest complete COCKROACH FOSSIL ever found (in an Ohio, U.S.A., coal mine) was mouse-size and from the CARBONIFEROUS PERIOD.

8 Contrary to scenes in the movie *JURASSIC PARK*, scientists have never been able to take DNA from bloodsucking INSECTS in amber.

9 The giant dragonfly relative, *MEGANEURA*, had a wingspan more than two feet (0.6 m) wide. Its name means "large-nerved" after veins in its wings.

10 At 8.2 feet (2.5 m) long, the sea scorpion *JAEKELOPTERUS* was bigger than a human. It may have been the LARGEST ARTHROPOD ever.

11 A 28-inch (71-cm)-long fossil of a Carboniferous-age land scorpion, *PULMONOSCORPIUS KIRKTONENSIS*, was found in Scotland.

12 GIANT ARTHROPODS might have SURVIVED IN CARBONIFEROUS TIMES because the air had more oxygen, keeping their huge bodies alive.

13 INSECTS WERE THE FIRST ANIMALS TO FLY. Their wings evolved 300 million years ago, helping them adapt to varied habitats.

14 FOSSILIZED BUTTERFLY WING SCALES can be collected from dissolved rock using a tool tipped with a human nose hair.

15 Scientists found a PREHISTORIC TICK trapped in amber. IT WAS ATTACHED TO A DINOSAUR FEATHER.

16 An AMBER-ENCASED TICK found in Costa Rica was FILLED WITH BLOOD, possibly from a monkey that plucked off the tick and dropped it.

17 A 100-million-year-old cockroach named *MANIPULATOR MODIFICAPUTIS* had long legs and big eyes, likely for chasing down prey.

18 The many-legged millipede *ARTHROPLEURA* was at least 6.6 feet (2 m) long. Its fossilized tracks are parallel rows of tiny prints.

35 CRAWLING FACTS ABOUT

An insect in amber found in the Dominican Republic

19 One fossil *ARTHROPLEURA* still had bits of its last meal in its stomach, showing that the millipede WAS A PLANT-EATER.

20 A piece of AMBER from the early Cretaceous period TRAPPED A YOUNG ORB-WEAVER SPIDER IN THE ACT OF EATING A WASP.

21 FOSSIL BEE and WASP NESTS often include plant material from the time they were built, giving CLUES TO THE ANCIENT ENVIRONMENT.

22 In 2018, German paleontologists USED X-RAYS TO FIND FOSSIL WASPS hiding within fossil flies, eating the flies from the inside out.

23 The Jurassic crustacean *DOLLOCARIS INGENS* had huge COMPOUND EYES. They took up a quarter of the eight-inch (20-cm) creature.

24 FOSSIL BARNACLES that were once stuck to ancient whales can tell scientists HOW THOSE WHALES MIGRATED.

25 The Triassic arthropod *AUSTROLIMULUS FLETCHERI,* from one fossil in Australia, had a BOOMERANG-SHAPED BODY.

26 Some shrimplike crustaceans called PHYLLOCARIDS reached jumbo size: They were UP TO 29.5 INCHES (75 cm) long.

27 OSTRACODS, bean-shaped crustaceans the size of a GRAIN OF SAND, appear in the fossil record from Cambrian to modern times.

28 Amber bought in a Myanmar market held *CHIMERARACHNE YINGI,* a new kind of Cretaceous arachnid with spiderlike legs.

29 SPIDERS were among the FIRST CREATURES TO WALK ON LAND. One kind had a long, scorpion-like tail.

30 Fossil wing scales show that BUTTERFLIES and MOTHS were AROUND BEFORE THERE WERE FLOWERS for them to pollinate.

31 COLLECTORS BEWARE! Sometimes forgers embed modern insects in fake amber and sell them as fossils.

32 ANTS were already underfoot when dinosaurs were walking on land. The earliest ants DATE BACK ABOUT 90 MILLION YEARS.

33 Giant insects died out during the GREAT DYING, the Permian-Triassic mass extinction 252 million years ago.

34 INSECTS GOT SMALLER as BIRDS EVOLVED, possibly because birds easily caught big, slow insects. Smaller, faster insects survived.

35 Part of a fossil pincer from a Silurian scorpion, *BRONTOSCORPIO ANGLICUS,* found in England, was the size of a dog.

EARLY INSECTS, SPIDERS, AND THEIR RELATIVES

1 Ancient organisms are often NAMED AFTER THEIR SHAPE, their BEHAVIOR, or after the PLACE where they were found.

2 When a fossil species is named, the namer must pick one fossil to be the best example. This is known as the TYPE SPECIMEN, or HOLOTYPE.

3 Scientific names for prehistoric life follow the same rules as those for modern creatures. THE GENUS AND SPECIES NAME MUST BE IN LATIN or at least follow Latin rules, such as *TYRANNOSAURUS REX*.

4 Prehistoric creatures usually keep the first name they were given, even if the name turns out to be mistaken. For instance *BASILOSAURUS,* MEANING "LIZARD KING," was originally thought to be a reptile, and kept its name after it was found to be a whale.

25 SCIENTIFIC FACTS ABOUT

5 THE QUICK WAY TO REFER TO A SCIENTIFIC NAME? Once the full name has been stated, experts use the first letter of the genus plus the species name: *T. rex,* for instance.

6 *BAMBIRAPTOR FEINBERGI,* a birdlike dinosaur discovered by a 14-year-old boy on his family's ranch, was named after Disney's Bambi because of its petite size.

7 Australian paleontologist Patricia Vickers-Rich named a BIG-EYED DINOSAUR she found *LEAELLYNASAURA* after her daughter, Leaellyn, and the "bird mimic" dinosaur *Timimus* after her son, Timothy.

8 Vickers-Rich also discovered a TWO-LEGGED DINOSAUR FOSSIL in Australia and called it *QANTASSAURUS* after the Australian airline Qantas.

11 Paleontologist David Martill got so annoyed by the difficulties of working with a new spinosaur skull that he named the animal *IRRITATOR CHALLENGERI.*

9 *THESCELOSAURUS NEGLECTUS,* the "neglected marvelous lizard" fossil, was kept in crates and ignored for years.

10 SMALL JURASSIC DINOSAUR *DRINKER NISTI* was named after, but not discovered by, paleontologist Edward Drinker Cope. Paleontologists may name their discoveries after the person who found the fossil or other experts they admire, but rarely after themselves.

12 *DRACOREX HOGWARTSIA,* a pachycephalosaur fossil in the Children's Museum of Indianapolis in Indiana, U.S.A., was NAMED IN HONOR OF THE HARRY POTTER BOOKS.

13 The trilobite *HAN SOLO* is the sole member of its genus, found in the Han ethnic region of China, and named for the *Star Wars* character.

14 According to a scientific paper by Eugene Gaffney, Pleistocene horned turtle *NINJEMYS OWENI* WAS NAMED AFTER "that totally rad, fearsome foursome epitomizing shelled success"—THE TEENAGE MUTANT NINJA TURTLES.

15 A Montana, U.S.A., horned ankylosaur with a clubbed tail was named *ZUUL CRURIVASTATOR* for the VILLAIN IN THE MOVIE *GHOSTBUSTERS.*

16 One microplankton is the size of a speck of dust, but it has one of the longest names: *PARVULARUGOGLOBIGERINA EUGUBINA.*

17 Jurassic dragonfly fossil *KIMMERIDGEBRACHYPTERAESCHNIDIUM ETCHESI* was found in Kimmeridge Bay in England and BELONGS TO THE FAMILY AESCHNIDIIDAE.

PREHISTORIC NAMES

18 A Chinese dinosaur embryo was nicknamed "BABY LOUIE" after its photographer, Louis Psihoyos. Its formal name is now *BEIBEILONG SINENSIS* ("baby dragon from China").

19 Some ancient lorikeets in the Marquesas Islands became extinct after humans arrived. One species was named *VINI VIDIVICI,* after the famous phrase from Roman general Julius Caesar: *"Veni, vidi, vici"*: "I came, I saw, I conquered."

20 Although he didn't find them, at least six prehistoric species are named after beloved naturalist David Attenborough, including the plesiosaur *ATTENBORO-SAURUS,* damselfly *MESOSTICTA DAVIDATTEN-BOROUGHI,* and tiny marsupial lion *Microleo attenboroughi.*

21 One doglike Eocene fossil was named *ARFIA.*

22 The person who discovered A TINY FOSSIL FLY wanted to name it I, but later changed it to *IYAIYAI,* pronounced ay-yai-yai!

23 *WAKIEWAKIE,* a prehistoric marsupial of Australia, was supposedly NAMED AFTER A LOCAL WAKE-UP CALL.

24 There are TRILOBITE SPECIES NAMED AFTER BEATLES Paul McCartney and George Harrison (*Struszia mccartneyi* and *S. harrisoni*), as well as the duo Simon and Garfunkel (*Avalanchurus simoni* and *A. garfunkeli*).

25 Paleontologist Edward Drinker Cope, who had many enemies, named a fossil mammal *ANISONCHUS COPHATER* for "THE NUMBER OF COPE-HATERS WHO SURROUND ME."

MANY FOSSIL SITES are in **DRY, ROCKY PLACES IN DIRECT SUNLIGHT.** From a campsite, **PALEONTOLOGISTS** set out every morning **WEARING BROAD-BRIMMED HATS** to protect against the burning sun and carrying lots and **LOTS OF WATER** and **HEAVY TOOLS.** Teams in the American West keep an eye out for rattlesnakes and scorpions as they hike.

? DID YOU KNOW?

ON A
DINOSAUR DIG

Digging up dinosaur fossils is hard work. At a site where fossils have been spotted in the ground—or where scientists know they'll find the right kind of fossil-bearing rocks—a team of paleontologists and volunteer diggers sets up camp.

Complete dinosaur skeletons aren't just lying around on the ground, waiting to be discovered. Most dino fossils are broken into pieces and scattered. Some will have exposed bits sticking out of the rock, with the rest of the bones buried deep. Paleontologists will map out the site and mark where they think fossils might be found, based on their experiences at other digs. Then they start removing the rock—called the overburden—that surrounds the bones. Sometimes this involves big, noisy tools such as jackhammers or saws. The closer the team gets to the fossil, the smaller the tools they use. Near a fossil bone, a digger will chip away with little picks and rock hammers, taking care not to scrape the fossil itself. As they work, paleontologists take notes about where the bones were found, which will help them understand how the animal died and what kind of environment it was buried in.

When the team has finished cutting closely around the fossil, they protect it with wet paper towels, toilet paper, or cloth. Then they label it and encase it with a plaster jacket, which will protect it when it is transported back to a laboratory to be studied.

To get close to this fossil, this paleontologist used a pick and brush to remove rocks and dirt.

1 **Pterosaurs** were not dinosaurs. They were **flying reptiles** that first appeared in the late Triassic, around the same time as the first dinosaurs.

2 **Pterosaur fossils are rare.** Their delicate, hollow bones didn't fossilize well.

3 Italian naturalist **Cosimo Collini discovered the first pterosaur in 1784,** but he thought it was a swimming animal with long flippers.

4 A fossil from Solnhofen, Germany, shows a pterosaur, *Rhamphorhynchus,* with its wings impaled by a large fish, *Aspidorhynchus.* The fish may have accidentally become tangled in the pterosaur's wings, dragging them both to the seafloor.

5 **Pterosaur wings** were supported by a very long finger bone—the **fourth finger on each arm.**

6 **Fossils of young pterosaurs** are called **flaplings.**

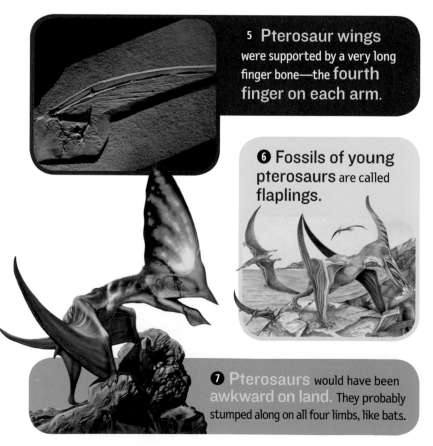

7 **Pterosaurs** would have been **awkward on land.** They probably stumped along on all four limbs, like bats.

PTEROSAURS

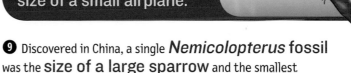

8 In 1971, a geology graduate student in Texas discovered the first *Quetzalcoatlus*, the biggest of all pterosaurs with a wingspan over 33 feet (10 m). **That's the size of a small airplane.**

9 Discovered in China, a single *Nemicolopterus* fossil was the **size of a large sparrow** and the smallest pterosaur yet found. It may be a youngster, not fully grown.

10 The fossil Pokémon character **Aerodactyl is based on pterosaurs.**

11 The *Pteranodon* is the official state flying fossil of Kansas, U.S.A.

12 Fossil *Pteranodon* have been **found in North American rocks that were once far out to sea.** The *Pteranodon* were probably hunting for fish among the waves.

13 A small pterosaur fossil discovered in 1971 had such fine detail that it revealed a hairlike covering on the animal's body. Named *Sordes pilosus* ("hairy devil"), the pterosaur may have been warm-blooded.

14 Giant pterosaurs called *Hatzegopteryx,* found on Hateg Island in Romania, may have been able to **prey on small dinosaurs.**

15 *Pteranodon* skulls had long, backward-pointing bony crests. Paleontologists aren't sure what they were for.

Some pterosaurs caught fish from ancient seas.

1 Swimming reptiles ICHTHYOSAURS, PLESIOSAURS, AND MOSASAURS hunted in the oceans at the same time that dinosaurs walked on land.

2 REPTILE SWIMMERS WERE AIR BREATHERS, so they must have come to the surface often to take in air.

3 The early turtles known as *ODONTOCHELYS* had shells on their bellies, but not on their backs.

4 A family of fossil hunters in Kansas, U.S.A., found the bones of a PREGNANT PLESIOSAUR. Its baby would have been about six feet (1.8 m) long at birth.

25 SCALY FACTS ABOUT

5 THE BIGGEST MOSASAURS could be UP TO 50 FEET (15 m) long.

6 ICHTHYOSAURS, DOLPHIN-LIKE MARINE REPTILES, started out as land animals. The bones of their four limbs evolved into flippers.

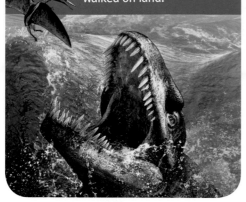

7 Chinese fossils include a mother ICHTHYOSAUR giving birth to a baby.

8 The first *MOSASAURUS* fossil, with a three-foot (0.9-m)-long jaw, became famous after it was FOUND IN THE NETHERLANDS in 1798. Invading French soldiers then stole it and took it to France.

9 A MOSASAUR FOSSIL found in Angola had three smaller mosasaurs in its gut.

10 MOSASAURS HAD DOUBLE-HINGED JAWS, like those of snakes. These reptiles may have started out as snakelike land animals before evolving into sea creatures.

11

MOSASAURS HAD TWO SETS OF TEETH in their upper jaws.

12 ROBERT DARWIN, the great-grandfather of famous naturalist Charles Darwin, DISCOVERED A FOSSIL PLESIOSAUR SKELETON in the early 18th century, although an expert identified it as a crocodile or porpoise.

13 A fossil *ALBERTONECTES* plesiosaur housed in Canada's Royal Tyrrell Museum has a **23-FOOT (7-M)-LONG NECK** with 76 vertebrae.

14 Early ICHTHYOSAURS had long, flexible skeletons, which may mean they swam by wiggling side to side like eels.

15 The crescent tails of later ICHTHYOSAURS are like those of today's tunas, so, like tunas, those reptiles **WERE PROBABLY SUPERFAST.**

16 FORTY FOSSIL ICHTHYOSAURS— one of North America's largest collections—were found buried in the ground next to the abandoned ghost town of Berlin, Nevada, U.S.A. They are now part of **BERLIN-ICHTHYOSAUR STATE PARK.**

18 ICHTHYOSAURS VANISH FROM THE FOSSIL RECORD BEFORE THE GREAT CRETACEOUS-PALEOGENE mass extinction. They may have died out due to competition from long-necked plesiosaurs, or because of environmental change.

17 The Triassic ichthyosaur *SHONISAURUS*, 55 feet (17 m) long, is **NEVADA'S STATE FOSSIL.**

SWIMMING REPTILES

19 ICHTHYOSAUR SKULLS HAVE HUGE EYE SOCKETS with rings of bone inside them. These "SCLERAL RINGS" probably protected the animals' enormous eyes from water pressure.

20 PLESIOSAURS ATE ICHTHYOSAURS. A fossil plesiosaur found in Wyoming, U.S.A., had a partly digested ichthyosaur fossil in its stomach.

21 Some ICHTHYOSAUR SKELETONS show bone damage due to THE BENDS, a sickness that comes from diving very deeply and rising rapidly in the sea.

22 Nicknamed "Eric," a fossil pliosaur found in Australia was **COVERED WITH OPALS, SEMIPRECIOUS GEMS.** Students raised $450,000 to keep Eric from being broken up and sold.

25 Some people claim that the mythical LOCH NESS MONSTER IS A PLESIOSAUR. However, plesiosaur necks weren't strong enough to rise out of the water in the classic curved Loch Ness pose.

23 The eye sockets of *OPHTHALMOSAURUS* ("eye lizard"), a large Jurassic ichthyosaur, are 9 inches (23 cm) across. **ITS EYES WOULD HAVE BEEN AS BIG AS BOWLING BALLS.**

24 In 2006, scientists on the Arctic island Svalbard found the fossil remains of a huge pliosaur. **ITS STRONG JAWS COULD HAVE BITTEN A SMALL CAR IN HALF.**

1 Germany has several great *LAGERSTÄTTEN*—extraordinary fossil sites—where **FINE MUDDY SEDIMENT TRAPPED ORGANISMS** at the bottom of ancient seas or lake beds.

2 People first dug up the **FOSSIL-RICH STONE IN SOLNHOFEN,** in southern Germany, because it was just right for making flat plates for printing books.

3 Solnhofen's fine-grained **JURASSIC LIMESTONE PRESERVES DELICATE DETAILS** that are usually lost in fossils.

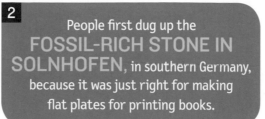

4 More than **600 DIFFERENT PREHISTORIC SPECIES** can be found at Solnhofen.

5 Solnhofen's rocks hold more than **50 SPECIES OF ANCIENT DRAGONFLIES.**

25 FACTS ABOUT FOSSIL HOT

6 Around 1874, Solnhofen yielded what may be the **WORLD'S MOST FAMOUS FOSSIL:** a beautifully feathered *ARCHAEOPTERYX,* now in a Berlin museum.

7 **SOLNHOFEN'S STONE** captures so many details that **EVEN THE INTERNAL ORGANS OF SOME FOSSILS CAN BE SEEN.**

8 More than **29 PTEROSAUR SPECIES** have been found at Solnhofen, including the rare, hawk-size *SCAPHOGNATHUS.*

9 A fossil found at Solnhofen was from a *GEOSAURUS,* A SHARP-TOOTHED, OCEAN-SWIMMING ANCESTOR of modern crocodiles.

10 **SOLNHOFEN'S QUARRIES** held a perfectly preserved **COELACANTH, A LOBE-FINNED FISH** that was thought to be extinct. Then a live one was discovered in the 20th century off South Africa.

11 **THE HUNSRÜCK SLATE MINES** in western Germany are famous for their detailed fossils from the **DEVONIAN PERIOD.**

12 More than 400 SPECIES OF UNDERWATER ORGANISMS have been found at Hunsrück, including trilobites, crinoids, and fish.

13 The HUNSRÜCK SLATE held the only known fossil of an ADULT SEA SPIDER, a long-legged, clawed, underwater arthropod.

14 The Hunsrück slate contained the nearly complete fossil of *DREPANASPIS,* A PRIMITIVE JAWLESS FISH with a mouth that opened up toward the top of its head.

15 THE FOSSIL-RICH MESSEL PIT, in central Germany, was almost made into a landfill in the 1970s before the government bought it and preserved it.

16 Germany's Messel Pit holds excellent FOSSILS AT LEAST 34 MILLION YEARS OLD, including early mammals.

17 LAND ANIMALS found at the Messel Pit may have been KILLED BY VOLCANIC GASES before falling into the lake and becoming preserved in the low-oxygen water at the bottom.

SPOTS: GERMANY

18 Some mammal fossils at Messel, such as the SQUIRREL-LIKE *KOPIDODON,* preserve the FINE DETAILS OF THEIR FUR.

19 A fossil JEWEL BEETLE found at Messel still had its original SHINY GREEN COLOR.

20 The detailed fossil of a CAT-SIZE HORSE ANCESTOR, *EUROHIPPUS MESSELENSIS,* was discovered at the Messel Pit with its unborn baby still inside it.

21 Complete with skin, fur, and stomach contents, a little *DARWINIUS MASILLAE* from the Messel Pit is one of the best primate fossils known. ITS NICKNAME IS "IDA."

22 A BIRD FOSSIL FOUND AT MESSEL with a small skull and strange bony knobs on its neck was named *PERPLEXICERVIX MICROCEPHALON,* or "incomprehensible neck tiny head."

23 Bird fossils from the Messel Pit include the "terror bird" *GASTORNIS,* taller than an adult man.

24 WELL-PRESERVED SKELETONS of Jurassic sea creatures and pterosaurs fill the POSIDONIA OIL SHALE formation in southwestern Germany.

25 PTEROSAUR FOSSILS found at Posidonia include *DORYGNATHUS,* an eagle-size flier with long, sharp fangs sticking out of its jaw.

THE DINOSAUR
FAMILY TREE

Dinosaurs evolved about 240 to 230 million years ago during the Triassic period. Their ancestors were small reptiles, hunters that ran on their hind legs. In the late Triassic, these fast-moving reptiles evolved into two groups of dinosaurs named for their hip bones. In saurischian, or lizard-hipped dinosaurs, one of the three hip bones points forward. In ornithischian, or bird-hipped dinosaurs, the same bone points backward.

Saurischian dinosaurs comprised all the meat-eaters, including tyrannosaurs and raptors, but also the huge, plant-eating sauropods. Ornithischians were all plant-eaters. Among them were such sturdy, four-legged dinosaurs as *Stegosaurus* and *Ankylosaurus*. The direct descendants of dinosaurs—birds—are still with us today. They didn't evolve from bird-hipped dinosaurs, though, but from feathered, lizard-hipped dinos.

Dinosaurs were truly successful animals. As continents moved and climates changed, they traveled and evolved into a wide range of shapes and sizes. In the end, they ruled Earth for more than 170 million years.

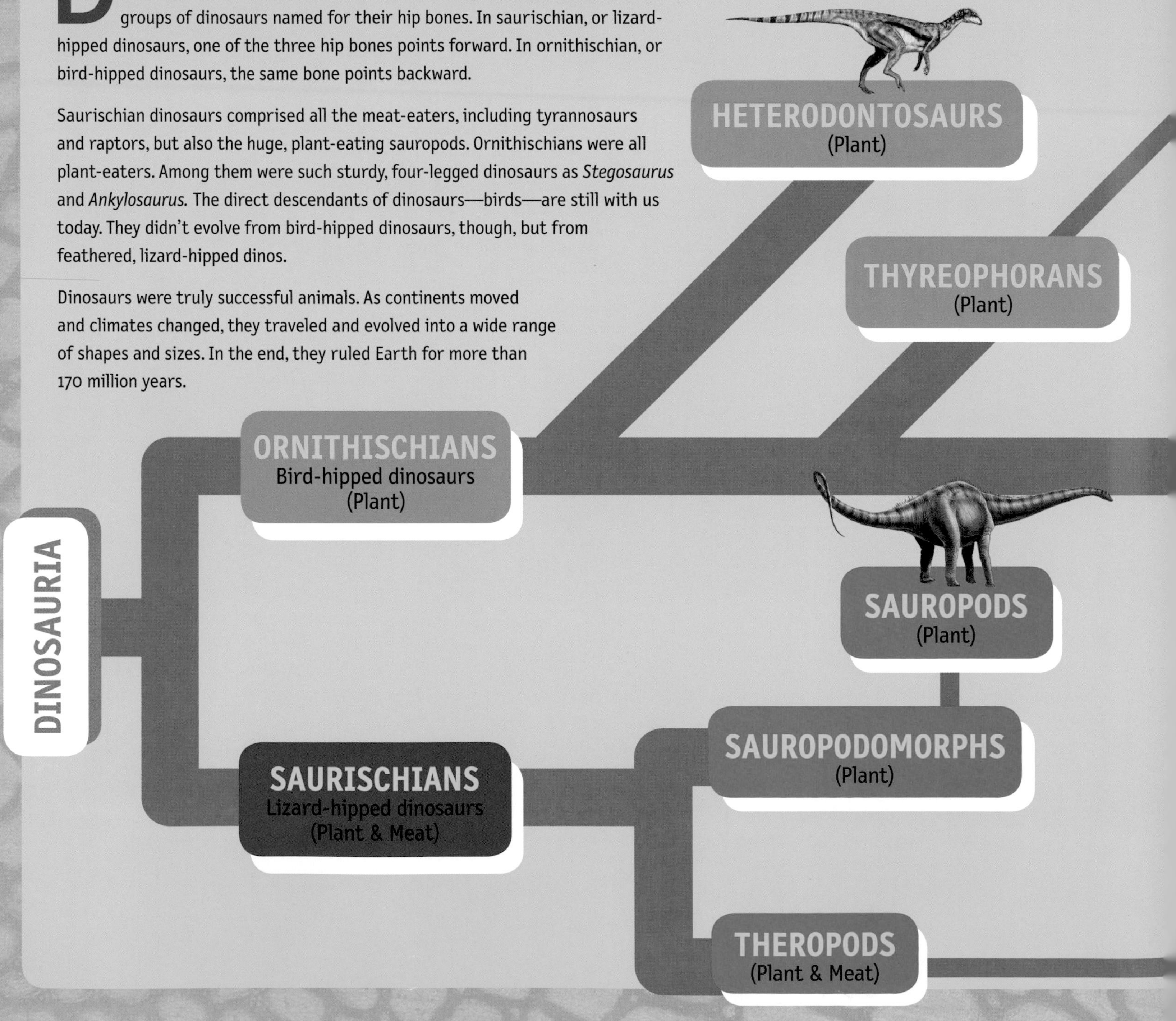

HETERODONTOSAURS
(Plant)

THYREOPHORANS
(Plant)

ORNITHISCHIANS
Bird-hipped dinosaurs
(Plant)

DINOSAURIA

SAUROPODS
(Plant)

SAUROPODOMORPHS
(Plant)

SAURISCHIANS
Lizard-hipped dinosaurs
(Plant & Meat)

THEROPODS
(Plant & Meat)

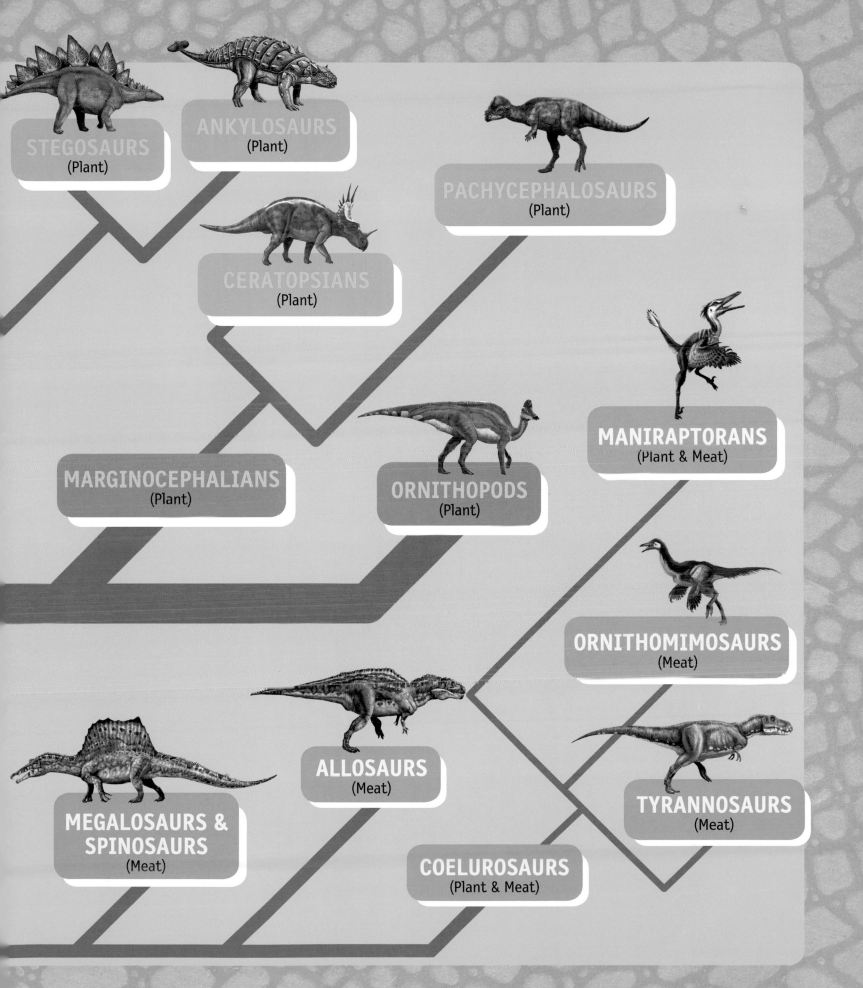

STEGOSAURS
(Plant)

ANKYLOSAURS
(Plant)

PACHYCEPHALOSAURS
(Plant)

CERATOPSIANS
(Plant)

MANIRAPTORANS
(Plant & Meat)

MARGINOCEPHALIANS
(Plant)

ORNITHOPODS
(Plant)

ORNITHOMIMOSAURS
(Meat)

ALLOSAURS
(Meat)

MEGALOSAURS &
SPINOSAURS
(Meat)

TYRANNOSAURS
(Meat)

COELUROSAURS
(Plant & Meat)

15 FAR-OUT FACTS ABOUT

1 Small, two-legged reptiles known as **archosaurs** were the direct ancestors of dinosaurs, crocodiles, and birds.

2 *Silesaurus,* found in Poland, was a close reptile ancestor of dinosaurs. It was a plant-eater that walked on all fours like a big dog.

NORTH AMERICA

SOUTH AMERICA AFRICA

ANTARCTICA AUSTRALIA

3 When dinosaurs first appeared on Earth, the continents where they lived were part of one big landmass called Pangaea.

4 *Nyasasaurus,* found in Tanzania, Africa, may be the earliest dinosaur ever found, dating back 240 million years. Scientists have only a partial skeleton, so they cannot be sure it's a dino.

5 *Eoraptor,* found in Argentina, appeared around 228 million years ago and was one of the earliest dinosaurs. **It was a small, sharp-toothed hunter** that ran on two legs.

6 *Eoraptor's* hands had five fingers. Later dinosaurs had up to four.

7 The scientific name *Eoraptor lunensis* means "dawn hunter from the Valley of the Moon."

8 *Herrerasaurus,* a big meat-eater found in Argentina, was one of the first dinos to have key dinosaur features, such as specialized hip bones.

THE FIRST DINOSAURS

9 *Herrerasaurus* had teeny arms but long hands.

10 *Riojasaurus,* found in South America, was the first giant dinosaur. About the size of a bus, the plant-eater had a skinny neck and tail but a heavy, bulky body and legs.

11 Well-preserved specimens of *Tawa hallae,* a human-size early predator, were found in a quarry at Ghost Ranch in New Mexico, U.S.A. Ancient floods may have piled up the bones before they were buried in the sediment.

12 Little *Eocursor,* found in South Africa, was one of the first bird-hipped dinosaurs. Its name means "dawn runner" because it was an early dino and because its long legs probably made it speedy.

13 The eight-foot (2.4-m)-long Triassic hunter *Coelophysis* had four fingers, but only three worked.

14 Many fossils of big Triassic plant-eaters known as *Plateosaurus* have been found in a quarry in Germany. Researchers think the animals might have waded into a swamp or river, become stuck in the mud, and drowned.

Plateosaurus tilted up on its hind legs to feed high in trees.

15 Plateosaurs traveled in herds, standing up on their sturdy hind legs to chomp leaves from trees.

1
PLANT-EATING DINOSAURS first appeared in the late Triassic period, about 220 MILLION YEARS AGO.

2
SAUROPODS, a group of plant-eating dinosaurs, were the biggest land animals ever. Some weighed as much as 11 elephants.

3
SAUROPODS HAD HUGE, HEAVY BODIES, LONG NECKS with SMALL HEADS, thick pillar-like legs, and long tails.

4
The 19th-century paleontologist OTHNIEL CHARLES MARSH came up with the name SAUROPOD. It means "LIZARD-FOOTED."

5
COMPLETE FOSSILS of sauropods, especially with skulls, ARE RARE. THE SKULLS WERE SMALL AND DELICATE.

6
DINOSAUR TRACKS show that many plant-eaters lived and MIGRATED IN HERDS, sometimes in groups of thousands.

7
PLANT-EATING DINOSAURS often HAD ARMOR or other defenses that would have helped defend them from meat-eating enemies.

8
In 1877, in Colorado, Marsh named a new sauropod skeleton *APATOSAURUS.* Later, he named the same kind of skeleton *BRONTOSAURUS.*

9
SAUROPODS were big, but they HAD SMALL BRAINS, about the size of two chicken eggs.

10
SAUROPODS swallowed their food WITHOUT CHEWING IT. Their huge gut gradually digested the food. (Don't try this yourself!)

11
REBBACHISAURUS, A GIANT SAUROPOD from Africa, had a long ridge along its back that may have helped the big animal cool off.

12
The huge sauropod *BRACHIOSAURUS* was AS HEAVY AS 11 ELEPHANTS. It was so weighty that it could only walk slowly, and couldn't run.

13
A *BRACHIOSAURUS'S* HEART would have WEIGHED 441 POUNDS (200 kg)—about as much as an upright piano.

14
The sauropod *SHUNOSAURUS* was FOUND BY STUDENTS in China in the 1970s. Later, workers dug up full skeletons, with club tails.

15
MAMENCHISAURUS, an enormous sauropod from China, was likely 115 feet (35 m) from head to tail, a third of a football field.

16
MAMENCHISAURUS had one of THE LONGEST NECKS OF ANY ANIMAL in history. It was as long as six giraffe necks end to end.

17
HUGE FOSSILS found in Colorado belonged to a new genus of sauropod, *SUPERSAURUS,* which could have been up to 112 feet (34 m) long.

18
An amateur fossil hunter in England found a bit of 133-MILLION-YEAR-OLD DINO BRAIN, possibly a plant-eater's, that showed blood vessels.

19
GIANT SAUROPODS needed giant amounts of food to survive. The biggest likely ate 1,000 pounds (454 kg) of plants each day.

20
DIPLODOCUS SKELETONS have long tails, with 80 vertebrae (spinal bones). The tails may have been cracked like a whip for defense.

35 ENORMOUS

21 The **BIGGEST SAUROPODS** are known as **TITANOSAURS**. Fossil titanosaurs have been **FOUND ALL OVER THE WORLD**.

22 A five-foot (1.5-m)-long thighbone, found in Egypt, belonged to a NEW SPECIES OF TITANOSAUR: *PARALITITAN*.

23 *SALTASAURUS* was a small titanosaur—just 42 feet (12.8 m) long—but fossil osteoderms, bony plates, show that it had thick, armored skin.

24 Fossil *SALTASAURUS* EGGS, found in Argentina, **HELD BABY DINOS** that already had armored skin.

25 Paleontologist Kenneth Lacovara estimated that his NEW TITANOSAUR would have been one of the biggest ever. He named it *DREADNOUGHTUS*: "fears nothing."

26 **FOSSIL JAWS** show that many long-necked dinosaurs had thin, **PENCIL-LIKE TEETH**, probably used to strip leaves from high branches.

27 Some dinosaur fossils have stones, known as **GASTROLITHS**, inside their rib cages. Swallowing stones may have helped dino stomachs grind up plants.

28 In 2005, an Australian man spotted the bones of a new kind of titanosaur: *SAVANNASAURUS ELLIOTTORUM*. He nicknamed it "Wade."

29 A rare fossil of a baby *RAPETOSAURUS*, found in Madagascar, shows the sauropod was dog-size at birth. Adults grew three times as tall as a giraffe.

30 The Pokémon Fossil characters **AMAURA** and **AURORUS** are based on the spiny sauropod *AMARGASAURUS*.

31 The sauropod *EUROPASAURUS*, found in Germany, may have been a DWARF SPECIES that evolved to be smaller over time as it lived on an island.

32 **SAUROPODS GREW FAST**. Some may have doubled their size in the first week and gained more than **2 TONS (1.8 T) A YEAR** in their youth.

33 The sauropod *JOBARIA*, which was discovered in Niger, in Africa, is named after Jobar, a giant creature from folktales.

34 Weighing perhaps 70 tons (64 t), the titanosaur *ALAMOSAURUS* may have been North America's heaviest dinosaur.

35 Most **SAUROPODS**, except for titanosaurs, died out before the **MASS EXTINCTION** that killed the last non-bird dinosaurs.

FACTS ABOUT GIANT PLANT-EATERS

A group of *Tenontosaurus* and *Argentinosaurus* migrates to find water.

15 FACTS ABOUT FOSSIL HOT

❶ The **Patagonia region** of Argentina, in South America's southern tip, is one of the **richest sources of dinosaur fossils in the world.** Dozens of new species have been discovered there.

2 **Fossils from Argentina** range from the **very first to the very last dinosaurs.**

❸ Argentina's hot, dry Ischigualasto formation holds some of the earliest dinosaurs, such as little *Eoraptor,* 228 million years old.

❹ The Ischigualasto formation is now a hot, dry desert, but fossil trees and ferns show that in prehistoric times it was green and rainy.

❺ **Herrerasaurs, early meat-eating dinos,** may have fought each other. One herrerasaur skull discovered in Argentina had bite marks that could have come from another herrerasaur.

❻ *Herrerasaurus* fossils were first discovered in Argentina's Ischigualasto formation by Victorino Herrera, a rancher.

❼ A Triassic dinosaur discovered in northwestern Argentina seems to be the earliest big sauropod, a massive plant-eater that would have weighed more than 11 tons (10 t)—as heavy as a massive anchor on an ocean liner. Its discoverers named it *Ingentia prima,* "first giant."

SPOTS: ARGENTINA

Meat-eating *Eoraptor* with a dicynodont— a mammal-like, plant-eating reptile too big for *Eoraptor* to attack

8 Argentina's dinosaur findings include the biggest plant-eater, *Argentinosaurus,* and one of the biggest meat-eaters, *Giganotosaurus.*

9 Most dinosaurs discovered in Argentina are different from those in North America because North and South America were not joined together for most of the time that dinosaurs walked on Earth.

10 Many fossils of *Scaphonyx,* a stocky dog-size reptile, have been found in the Ischigualasto formation, showing that they lived side by side with early dinosaurs.

11 Paleontologist Alfred Romer described the area of Ischigualasto as "the most extraordinary fossil cemetery ever imagined." It covers 233 square miles (604 sq km) of northwestern Argentina.

12 Based on a skull found in Argentina's Anacleto formation, *Abelisaurus* was a 30-foot (9-m)-long dinosaur that might have had crests rising above its eyes.

13 Found only in Argentina, the two-ton (1.8-t) plant-eater *Ischigualastia* might have been prey for the biggest local meat-eaters, such as *Herrerasaurus.*

14 Fossils of *Mapusaurus,* a huge predatory dinosaur, were found in groups of adults and youngsters in Argentina's Huincul formation. This may mean that they hunted together.

15 Scientists have found only one, partial, broken-up skeleton of *Pisanosaurus* in Argentina. They aren't sure if the three-foot (1-m)-long creature was an early dinosaur or a reptile relative.

No one has found any ARGENTINOSAURUS EGGS so far, but they were PROBABLY A BIT BIGGER THAN A BOWLING BALL. Babies would have started out small, but they kept growing their entire lives. As big as they were, these sauropods may have had enemies almost as large. HUGE PREDATORS such as GIGANOTOSAURUS or MAPUSAURUS might have HUNTED THEM IN PACKS and taken them down.

ARGENTINOSAURUS

In 1987, Guillermo Heredia discovered what he thought was a big piece of driftwood on his sheep ranch in Argentina. It turned out to be something much more exciting. Heredia had found the first known fossil—a shinbone—of what may have been the biggest dinosaur ever, *Argentinosaurus*.

We still don't know exactly what the dinosaur looked like, because only backbones, ribs, and the shinbone have ever been found. However, by studying those fossils and comparing them to similar dinosaurs, paleontologists José Bonaparte and Rodolfo Coria were able to put together a description of this huge animal and name it *Argentinosaurus*, or "Argentina lizard."

Argentinosaurus was a titanosaur, the largest kind of sauropod, which was a long-necked, plant-eating dinosaur. It may have been 100 feet (30 m) long and could have weighed as much as 100 tons (91 t)—as much as 20 elephants. This would make it the largest animal ever to walk on land. Thundering along in herds, the giant beasts would have traveled at only about five miles an hour (8 km/h). Like other sauropods, they would have stretched out their long necks to eat leaves from the tops of trees.

Argentinosaurus **stood more than 20 feet (6 m) high.**

15 PIERCING FACTS ABOUT

1 **Stegosaurs** and their relatives were massive plant-eaters of the late Jurassic period. Armored skin and spikes helped protect them against the **meat-eating dinos** that shared their world.

2 In the 19th century, paleontologist Othniel Charles Marsh decided that a big opening in a *Stegosaurus* fossil spine meant that it had a second brain near its tail. This was wrong, but the **"brain in the butt"** idea lasted until recent times.

3 Fossil footprints suggest that **stegosaurs** may have **traveled in family groups.**

4 **Stegosaurs had spiky tails** that might have been used as weapons. Fossils show damage to the tails that might have come from fighting.

5 Complete *Stegosaurus* fossils **are rare.** Museums often have to build fossil skeletons out of several separate animals.

6 The bony plates sticking out of a stegosaur's back weren't attached to its skeleton. They grew directly out of the dinosaur's skin.

7 Marsh, who discovered *Stegosaurus,* originally thought that it walked on two legs, because its front legs were so short.

SPIKY DINOSAURS

Ankylosaurus attacks a giant crocodile with its massive club tail.

8 Paleontologists aren't sure what the plates on a *Stegosaurus*'s back were for. They may have helped cool the animal, or they may have attracted mates.

9 Ankylosaurs were plant-eating dinosaurs that could be the size of tanks. They were slow, but they were protected by tough, armorlike skin.

10 Predators would want to back off from *Ankylosaurus*. It had a club at the end of its tail made of osteoderms, special bones that form in the skin.

11 Ankylosaur fossils are usually found on their backs. Scientists think this is because their dead bodies filled with air and flipped upside down in the water.

12 The ankylosaur *Gastonia burgei* had five pairs of big triangular spikes sticking out behind its shoulders.

13 *Minmi,* found in Australia, was a small ankylosaur, but what it lacked in size, it made up in defenses. This bear-size dino was covered in plates, spikes, and armored patches.

14 The ankylosaur *Tarchia,* found in Mongolia, had a large triangular head covered with bony lumps and spikes. It might have been pretty smart—its brain was twice as big as those of similar dinosaurs found nearby.

15 Miners at the oil sands of northern Alberta, Canada, found the most complete fossil ever of a nodosaur, a plant-eating dinosaur. Its spiky, armored skin and head were perfectly preserved.

1 CERATOPSIANS were CRETACEOUS PLANT-EATERS with beaky mouths and bony frills and horns on their skulls. The word "ceratopsian" means "horned face."

2 Scientists think that the HORNS AND FRILL on ceratopsian heads were mainly for SHOWING OFF TO OTHER DINOSAURS, NOT FOR FIGHTING.

3 The earliest known ceratopsian is THE DOG-SIZE CHAOYANGSAURUS, which lived in the late Jurassic period.

4 *Styracosaurus* was a pointy wonder. Its frilled skull had a big nose spike and four or more spikes around the edges. STYRACOSAURUS means "SPIKED LIZARD."

5 The jaws of the dog-size dinosaur PSITTACOSAURUS had sharp, curved beaks like those of a parrot—which is why it is named "PARROT LIZARD."

25 FRILLED FACTS ABOUT

6 PSITTACOSAURUS might have had quills or bristles growing out of its back.

7 TRICERATOPS was the BIGGEST HORNED DINOSAUR. It could grow to 30 feet (9 m) long and weighed more than 12,000 pounds (5,443 kg)—as heavy as an African elephant.

8 TRICERATOPS chewed up tough plants using 800 LITTLE TEETH.

9 TRICERATOPS WAS PIGEON-TOED. When it walked, its toes pointed inward.

10 TRICERATOPS had one of THE BIGGEST SKULLS of any land animal. The largest skull yet found is 8.2 feet (2.5 m) long.

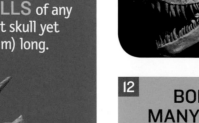

11 TRICERATOPS dinos were big, but their ENEMIES WERE BIGGER. Some *Triceratops* fossils have bite marks that seem to have come from *Tyrannosaurus rex* teeth.

12 BONE BEDS, areas where the earth is FILLED WITH MANY BONES OR FOSSILS, show that ceratopsians, such as *Triceratops*, lived in family herds. They may have huddled in a circle, horns out, to defend themselves against enemies.

13
A CERATOPSIAN'S BONY HORNS might have been COVERED IN KERATIN, the same kind of tough material that makes up your fingernails.

14
TRICERATOPS HORRIDUS is the state fossil of South Dakota, U.S.A.

15
Some ceratopsians were petite. A GRACILICERATOPS fossil, found in Mongolia, was only the SIZE OF A CAT.

16
PACHYCEPHALOSAURUS skulls are almost nine inches (23 cm) thick. The scientific name means "THICK-HEADED LIZARD."

17
PACHYCEPHALOSAURUS may have fought others of its kind by WHACKING THEM IN THE SIDE OF THE HEAD.

18
The ceratopsian ZUNICERATOPS CHRISTOPHERI was discovered by and named after eight-year-old Christopher Wolfe in New Mexico, U.S.A.

TRICERATOPS AND FAMILY

19
TRICERATOPS and PACHYCEPHALOSAURS WERE AMONG THE LAST DINOSAURS. They would have been walking on Earth until the mass dinosaur extinction about 65 million years ago.

20
Cat-size MICROPACHYCEPHALOSAURUS ("TINY THICK-HEADED LIZARD") was thought to be a tiny pachycephalosaur because the Chinese scientist who found it described a very thick skull. However, no one can find the skull anymore. The creature may be a ceratopsian, related to Triceratops.

21
PENTACERATOPS ("FIVE-HORNED FACE") did in fact have five horns around its huge, frilled skull. They may have been too thin and breakable to be weapons.

22

Two potential species, named DRACOREX and STYGIMOLOCH, may be young versions of Pachycephalosaurus. Scientists think that the animals' skulls changed a lot as they grew.

23
PACHYCEPHALOSAURUS'S EYES were set forward in its skull, which would have given it good THREE-DIMENSIONAL VISION.

24
PALEONTOLOGISTS found a FOSSILIZED NEST OF PROTOCERATOPS youngsters in THE GOBI IN ASIA. The little creatures might have been BURIED BY A SANDSTORM.

25
The ceratopsian EINIOSAURUS had a big, forward-curving horn, like a claw, on its nose.

1 The big Cretaceous plant-eater *Iguanodon* was one of the **first dinosaurs ever discovered.** Its teeth were found by English doctor Gideon Mantell in England and described in 1825.

2 *Iguanodon* may have **walked on two legs** at some times, and on **all four limbs** at other times.

3 *Iguanodon* fossils have been found on every continent except Antarctica.

4 *Iguanodon* hands have a sharp, spiky thumb that sticks out to the side. The spike might have been used for defense or for cutting up plants.

5 Hadrosaurs, Cretaceous plant-eaters, are often called **"duck-billed" dinosaurs** because their skulls had long, flat snouts like duck beaks.

6 Some hadrosaurs had crests curving out of the top of their heads.

7 Some **duck-billed dinosaurs** had more than **1,000 sharp little teeth.** They probably needed them to chew evergreen leaves.

IGUANODON AND FAMILY

8 George and Levi Sternberg found the famous "Trachodon mummy" fossil, a hadrosaur, in Wyoming, U.S.A., in 1908. The skeleton's bones were still attached to each other, and the body was covered with scaly skin.

9 Skulls of the dinosaur *Parasaurolophus,* a duck-billed dinosaur, **have a hollow tubelike crest.** A paleontologist modeled the crest out of bathroom tubing and found out that it would have made a tuba-like sound when the dinosaur blew through its nose.

10 Fossils found in the **"Dragon's Tomb"** bone bed in Mongolia in the 1950s include detailed impressions of bumpy hadrosaur skin.

11 Paleontologists discovered fossilized nests, eggs, and babies of *Maiasaura* dinosaurs in Montana, U.S.A., in the 1970s. Because the helpless babies would have needed a parent's care, the discovery showed that some dinosaurs **raised and fed their young.**

12 *Maiasaura* means **"good mother lizard."**

13 Hadrosaur fossils tell paleontologists that the animals' jaws could **chew tough plants** and move up and down, front to back, and side to side.

14 North America's *Edmontosaurus* was one of the **biggest hadrosaurs,** up to 42 feet (13 m) long—as big as a bus! It may have had a little crest on its head, like a rooster's.

15 Edmontosaurs traveled in big herds. Sometimes they were attacked by predators such as tyrannosaurs.

Parasaurolophus lived on an inland seaway that covered part of North America.

❶ Because of limited resources and time, The Museum of the Rockies in Montana, U.S.A, **only excavate fossils** if they find more than three bones together, or a skull, eggs, or nests.

❷ Fossil preparators—people who clean, repair, and mount fossils—are still working on some fossils collected in the last century and stored in museum basements.

❸ Fossilized bones taken from the ground are usually **protected in plaster casts** before they are sent to laboratories to be studied.

❹ When fossils arrive in a lab, preparators carefully cut away their plaster coverings to reveal the fossil surrounded by rock.

❺ Every fossil in a museum or lab is labeled with a catalog number and listed in a database.

035 001 65

❻ Preparators sometimes use tiny jackhammers, sandblasters, and dental tools to remove the rock from around a fossil.

❼ Preparators often coat a fossil with a special glue to strengthen it and hold it together.

ASSEMBLING SKELETONS

8 Tiny teeth and jaws are common microfossils. Paleontologists typically wash and sift many pounds of gravelly rock through a sieve to separate each of these fossils from its surroundings.

9 As paleontologists put together fossil skeletons, they compare them to modern-day animals, such as bears or crocodiles, to figure out how the prehistoric creature stood and moved.

10 Museums often make casts of bones by covering them with liquid rubber. After the rubber hardens, it is removed and filled with plaster or a plastic-y resin to make a model of the bone.

11 It took four years for paleontologists to dig the skeleton of a baby *Pentaceratops* out of the ground in New Mexico, U.S.A. A National Guard Blackhawk helicopter then airlifted the encased fossil to a museum in Albuquerque.

12 Complete skeletons made of real bones are rarely shown in museums—they are too valuable. Sophie the *Stegosaurus* at London's Natural History Museum is one of the few (almost complete) real skeletons on display.

13 Twelve preparators took 20,000 hours to put together Sue, the famous *T. rex* in the Field Museum in Chicago, Illinois, U.S.A.

14 To put together a 122-foot (37-m)-long titanosaur, workers at the American Museum of Natural History made 3D scans of its bones. Then they made casts of its skeleton with fiberglass and pieced them together over six months.

15 Fossilized bones sometimes have marks that show where muscles attached, which helps scientists know how to put the skeleton together.

Skeleton of *Tyrannosaurus rex*, whose name means "king of the tyrant lizards"

1 Because **FOSSIL ANIMALS ARE OFTEN INCOMPLETE**— and scientists are always finding new ones—prehistoric records of the biggest, smallest, oldest, and newest animals often change as new information comes in.

2 *LEEDSICHTHYS,* from the Jurassic period, may have been the biggest fish that ever lived, at about 55 feet (17 m) long—longer than a tractor trailer. One tailbone fossil alone is nine feet nine inches (3 m) wide.

3 The biggest crocodile ever was the Triassic reptile *Sarcosuchus,* nicknamed **"SUPERCROC."** It grew to 40 feet (12 m) long— as large as a modern school bus.

4 **THE OLDEST FOSSILS EVER FOUND ARE TINY MICROBES** in structures called stromatolites, found in west Australian rocks. They date back almost 3.5 billion years, to the early days of life on Earth.

5 *HADROCODIUM* may have been the **SMALLEST PREHISTORIC MAMMAL.** It was about the size of a paper clip.

25 TOP FACTS ABOUT

6 The four-winged *MICRORAPTOR* was probably the **LIGHTEST DINOSAUR,** weighing about two pounds (0.9 kg)— as much as two footballs.

7 The skeleton of a **122-FOOT (37-M) TITANOSAUR— LONGER THAN A BLUE WHALE** and likely the largest creature to walk on Earth—was put together for the American Museum of Natural History and is so long that it stretches across two rooms.

8 *SPINOSAURUS* may have been the **LONGEST MEAT-EATING DINOSAUR** from nose to tail tip. Estimates of its size range from 41 to 59 feet (12.5 to 18 m) long, almost as long as two telephone poles end to end.

9 The largest bird skull ever found comes from *KELENKEN GUILLERMOI,* a huge flightless **"TERROR BIRD"** from the Miocene epoch. The hook-shaped beak alone is 18 inches (46 cm) long.

10 Paleontologists in Saskatchewan, Canada, found what may be the **LARGEST COPROLITE** (piece of dinosaur poop) **EVER DISCOVERED.** The fossilized specimen was 17 inches (43 cm) long and may have come from a *T. rex.*

11 Scientists think an **ENORMOUS JAWBONE** found in England may have come from the **BIGGEST ICHTHYOSAUR EVER DISCOVERED,** a 85-foot (26-m)-long reptile.

12 A giant sauropod footprint in Australia is the **BIGGEST DINO TRACK** discovered. At five feet nine inches (1.8 m), an adult man could lie down inside it.

13 The big sauropod **BRACHIOSAURUS** was probably **THE TALLEST DINOSAUR.** It could raise its head, on a long neck, about 43 feet (13 m) from the ground.

14 About 20 inches (51 cm) long, **BEIBEILONG EGGS** first found by a Chinese farmer in the 1990s are the **LARGEST DINOSAUR EGGS** ever discovered—about as long as a newborn baby.

15 Preserved in the **LA BREA TAR PITS,** American lions were probably the biggest cats ever, at 8.2 feet (2.5 m) long and up to 1,153 pounds (523 kg).

16 Based on a leg fossil found in Argentina, paleontologists believe the massive **ARCTOTHERIUM** was the **BIGGEST BEAR** ever, weighing up to 3,856 pounds (1,749 kg). That's as much as a big car.

17 A complete skeleton hasn't been found yet, but the **PLEISTOCENE ELEPHANT** **PALAEOLOXODON NAMADICUS** may have been the largest land mammal. It would have stood 17.1 feet (5.2 m) tall at the shoulder—as high as the head of a giraffe—and weighed 24.3 tons (22 t).

PREHISTORIC RECORD HOLDERS

18 **THE BIGGEST RODENT** in history was **JOSEPHOARTIGASIA MONESI,** a Pliocene mammal about 10 feet (3 m) long and weighing up to 3,382 pounds (1,534 kg). Its front teeth were more than 12 inches (30 cm) long.

19 The **SMALLEST ARTHROPOD FOSSIL EVER** found was a **50-MILLION-YEAR-OLD MITE** found on a spider fossil. It was just .008 inches (0.2 mm) long—barely visible without a microscope.

20 The 100-ton (91-t) **ARGENTINOSAURUS** **MAY HAVE BEEN THE HEAVIEST DINOSAUR EVER,** but *Amphicoelias fragillimus* could have been bigger, at 190 feet (58 m) long and 135 tons (122 t). However, most of the bones of this sauropod have been lost, so we can't be sure.

21 Rib and spinal bone fossils found in Colombia came from the biggest snake ever found, named **TITANOBOA,** or **"TITANIC BOA."** It would have been 42.6 feet (13 m) long—longer than a telephone pole—and weighed 2,500 pounds (1,134 kg).

22 It is hard to guess at prehistoric speeds, but the **OSTRICH-LIKE ORNITHOMIMIDS** had long, powerful legs that might have allowed them to **SPRINT AT UP TO 40 MILES AN HOUR** (64 km/h).

23 In 1998, paleontologists in Wyoming, U.S.A., dug up the biggest dinosaur foot ever found, a **BRACHIOSAUR** fossil about 3.2 feet (1 m) wide. Of course, they nicknamed the fossil **"BIGFOOT."**

24 Preserved in an Illinois, U.S.A., coal mine is the **WORLD'S LARGEST FOSSILIZED WILDERNESS—** four square miles (10 sq km) of 307-million-year-old trees, leaves, and ferns.

25 Most fossil brachiopods (shelled marine animals) are about the size of a quarter, but record-setting **GIGANTOPRODUCTUS GIGANTEUS** was about one foot (30 cm) wide.

1
Meat-eating dinosaurs, known as theropods, evolved from little hunters like *Eoraptor* into giant predators such as *Giganotosaurus*— then into birds.

5
Many **theropods had feathers, but** none could fly.

9
Meat-eating dinosaurs lived beside plant-eaters for all of dinosaur time, from the late Triassic to the late Cretaceous periods.

13
Little *Troodon* **had one of the biggest brains,** compared to body size, of any dinosaur.

17
Contrary to the movie *Jurassic Park*, fossils show that *Dilophosaurus* **had a double crest** on its head, not its neck.

2
Fossils of **meat-eating dinosaurs have hollow, thin-walled bones.**

6
Meat-eaters typically had two strong hind legs for running **and two shorter front limbs** with claws for tearing apart prey.

10
Meat-eating dinos were probably scavengers as well as predators, eating dead animals they found.

14
The ridge on the back of *Cryolophosaurus's* skull, which scientists thought resembled singer Elvis Presley's pointy hairdo, led to its **nickname of "Elvisaurus."**

18
An *Aucasaurus* **skull** found in Argentina had damage possibly from **an attack** by another dinosaur.

3
Most theropods had sharp claws and sharp, curved teeth.

7
Fossil tracks of theropods are usually triangular and three-toed, with claws at the toe tips.

15
In 1991, geologist William Hammer found the skull of *Cryolophosaurus* on an icy mountain in Antarctica. It was the **first meat-eating dinosaur** found on that continent.

19
Carnotaurus, a predator from Argentina, **had two triangular horns** on its skull, likely used as weapons. Its name means **"meat-eating bull lizard."**

11
The fossil record shows that as **theropods** evolved, their **brains got bigger.**

4
Scientists have **found more fossils of plant-eating dinosaurs** than of meat-eaters.

8
Theropod teeth typically have jagged edges, like those on steak knives, that would have helped them tear into meat.

12
The front limbs of theropods were short and stiff and their hands and wrists probably couldn't roll or twist.

16
Eoraptor was small but fast. It may have hunted tiny mammals about the size of mice.

20
Carnotaurus was 25 feet (7.6 m) from head to tail, but it had tiny front limbs and hands.

50 FEARSOME Facts About MEAT-EATERS

70-million-year-old fossils of *Tyrannosaurus rex* and *Triceratops*

21
A cast of a complete *Coelophysis* skeleton is mounted inside New York City's 81st Street subway station.

22
More than 100 *Coelophysis* skeletons were found piled up at New Mexico's Ghost Ranch quarry.

23
The fierce, sail-backed *Spinosaurus* paddled in water with **ducklike feet.**

24
The skull of *Yangchuanosaurus*, a big predator found in China, was 3.6 feet (1.1 m) long. Its **forward-facing eyes** meant it had good hunting vision.

25
Dinosaur tracks found in Texas, U.S.A., in 1938 show where a predatory dinosaur, probably the 40-foot (12-m)-long *Acrocanthosaurus*, attacked a big sauropod.

26
Giganotosaurus was huge, but studies show that its **brain was the size of a banana.**

27
Giganotosaurus was among the **heaviest meat-eaters,** at 10 tons (9 t).

28
The first *Giganotosaurus* fossil was found by a fossil hunter driving a dune buggy across the desert in Argentina.

29
Baryonyx was a big meat-eater, but it also ate fish. A fossil was found with fish scales in its stomach.

30
The first *Spinosaurus* fossils were destroyed in World War II, when bombs blew up a museum in Munich, Germany. Later, a new partial skeleton was found in North Africa.

31
Based on studies of the legs and snout of a recently discovered *Spinosaurus* fossil, the huge dinosaur may have spent much of its time in the water.

32
Carcharodontosaurus was one of the **biggest predators** ever. At 45 feet (14 m) long, it had jagged, 6-inch (15-cm) teeth.

33
Based on a single incomplete skeleton from Mongolia, the chicken-size *Parvicursor* may have been one of the **smallest dinosaurs ever.**

34
In 1940, a Navajo man named Jesse Williams found the first skeletons of *Dilophosaurus* on a Navajo Reservation in Arizona, U.S.A.

35
The fourth skeleton of *Dilophosaurus* found in the American Southwest showed the distinctive double crests on its skull.

36
Eleven-year-old Jacob Walen of the Netherlands found the jawbone of a *Torvosaurus*, a two-ton (1.8-t) predator, during a family trip to Portugal in 2003.

37
The most complete skeleton of an Australian predatory dinosaur **belongs to** *Australovenator,* a theropod 16 feet (5 m) long.

38
Aucasaurus might have liked **eggs** for breakfast. One fossil was found on a sauropod nest filled with fossilized eggs.

39
Coelophysis was a speedy little **meat-eater** from the Triassic. It is one of the oldest dinosaurs for which we have full skeletons.

40
The fossil record shows that **meat-eating dinosaurs'** hands evolved from having five fingers to three.

41
Only one skeleton exists for fast, goose-size *Segisaurus*, a **theropod** found in Arizona in 1933.

42
A horned *Carnotaurus* skeleton found in Argentina had **scaly skin** with rows of raised knobs running down its back.

43
African theropod *Suchomimus*'s name means "crocodile mimic."

44
A fossilized imprint in Germany shows that a 150-million-year-old *Sciurumimus* theropod had a fluffy, squirrel-like tail.

45
Discovered in Mongolia, the skinny, bird-like theropod *Mononykus* had tiny arms that ended with a single claw.

46
Megalosaurus is the first dinosaur to be mentioned in literature, in Charles Dickens's 1852 novel *Bleak House*.

47
Mapusaurus, found in Argentina, was huge, the size of *Giganotosaurus*.

48
Herrerasaurus skulls had a flexible jaw joint for opening their mouths wide, like lizards, to swallow big prey.

49
Acrocanthosaurus, found in North America, was one of the **biggest meat-eaters,** but its big thighs and a heavy tail likely made it slow-moving.

50
Ceratosaurus nasicornis was three times the size of an adult man. It had two horns over its eyes and a horn on its nose, earning its name: "horned lizard nose horn."

1 TYRANNOSAURS were a group of strong, PREDATORY DINOSAURS that lived on most continents of the world from the late Jurassic to the late Cretaceous period.

2 TYRANNOSAURUS REX (T. rex) is the MOST FAMOUS tyrannosaur, but at least 25 species walked on Earth in prehistoric times.

3 TYRANNOSAURS typically had BIG, NARROW SKULLS, small forearms that ended in two or three fingers, and big hind limbs.

4 Some early tyrannosaurs were RELATIVELY SMALL. DILONG PARADOXUS, found in China, was about 6.5 feet (2 m) long.

5 Some fossils of DILONG PARADOXUS show signs of feathers on the jaw and tail.

25 TERRIFYING FACTS ABOUT

6 Studies of T. rex leg bones show it could RUN ABOUT 12 MILES an hour (19 km/h). A fast human could probably outrun it.

7 The Pokémon fossils TYRUNT and TYRANTRUM were inspired by Tyrannosaurus rex.

8 T. REX JAWS COULD BITE WITH 7,800 POUNDS (3,538 kg) of force. That's the weight of three small cars.

9 ALLOSAURS WERE BIG PREDATORS from the American West. With their huge skulls and short arms, they looked like tyrannosaurs but belonged to a different group of dinosaurs.

10 Scars on some skull fossils show that allosaurs and TYRANNOSAURS SOMETIMES BIT EACH OTHER on the face.

11 "Big Al," an unusually complete ALLOSAURUS FRAGILIS skeleton dug up in Wyoming, U.S.A., in the 1990s, had infections in its bones that might have led to its death.

12 Even though ALLOSAURUS HAD A BIG JAW that opened wide, studies show that it did not have a strong bite. Instead, allosaurs may have swung their jaws down like clubs to chomp their prey.

13 ALLOSAURS may have **HUNTED IN SMALL PACKS** for their prey.

14 Fossils found on a farm in Argentina in 2005 turned out to be a new and huge tyrannosaur. Named *TYRANNOTITAN,* it would have been up to 40 feet (12 m) long and weighed about 7.7 tons (7 t).

15 Some *T. rex* bones in museums have big tooth marks—marks that could only have been made by another *T. rex*. It seems the **BIG PREDATORS ATE THEIR RIVALS** after they killed them.

16 When paleontologists in Argentina found a **GIANT CURVED CLAW,** 12 inches (30 cm) long, they thought it must have come from a raptor foot. They named the dinosaur *MEGARAPTOR,* but now we know it was not a raptor, but a tyrannosaur-like beast, perhaps 26 feet (8 m) long.

17 Studies of *DASPLETOSAURUS* skulls suggest that tyrannosaurs didn't have lips. Their scaly jaws were more like those of crocodiles.

TYRANNOSAURS AND ALLOSAURS

18 *ALBERTOSAURUS,* a smaller relative of *T. rex,* apparently **TRAVELED IN PACKS.** Paleontologist Philip Currie discovered fossils of up to 26 albertosaurs together in one Canadian bone bed.

19 A *T. REX* **COPROLITE— FOSSILIZED POOP—** found in Canada was full of bone fragments from another dinosaur the *T. rex* had eaten.

20 Only a few young *T. REX* SPECIMENS have ever been found.

21 Discovered at a Chinese construction site, the tyrannosaur fossil *QIANZHOUSAURUS* was nicknamed "Pinocchio rex" because of its long, skinny snout.

22 A new tyrannosaur was discovered as a partial skeleton in New Mexico in 2012. Named *DYNAMOTERROR DYNASTES,* the 30-foot (9.1-m)-long predator was an early member of the tyrannosaur group, **DATING BACK 80 MILLION YEARS.**

23 Each of *T. REX'S* **SMALL ARMS** was probably strong enough to **LIFT 400 POUNDS** (181 kg).

24 The Mongolian tyrannosaur, *TARBOSAURUS BATAAR,* had even tinier arms, relative to its body, than its cousin *T. rex*. With its big jaws, however, it could easily overpower smaller animals.

25 Paleontologists have not found any *T. REX* EGGS yet— but they're still looking!

TYRANNOSAURUS REX

The fearsome, bigheaded, stumpy-armed *Tyrannosaurus rex* is probably the best known of all the dinosaurs. Legendary fossil collector Barnum Brown found the first partial skeleton of a *T. rex* in Wyoming, U.S.A., in 1900. Today, the remains of about 50 *T. rexes* have been found, although only a few skeletons are close to being complete.

We now know that *Tyrannosaurus rex* was the biggest member of a family of fierce meat-eaters called tyrannosaurids that lived in North America and Asia. Measuring about 40 feet (12 m) long from head to tail, *T. rex* weighed as much as an African elephant. It had a huge skull with a big brain. Its powerful jaws had 60 curved teeth, some up to one foot (30 cm) long. With these jaws, *T. rex* ripped hundreds of pounds of meat and bone from prey at one time and swallowed it whole. Big, muscular hind legs carried its massive body, but its tiny front arms still puzzle scientists. They were strong, but so short that they could not have pulled down prey. A heavy tail stuck out behind *T. rex* and balanced its heavy upper body as it ran.

Tyrannosaurus rex was the top predator in what is now the western United States and Canada during the late Cretaceous period. It would have ruled over the landscape until the moment when the Cretaceous-Paleogene extinction wiped out the last non-bird dinosaurs.

Tyrannosaurus rex hunts for food as *Quetzalcoatlus* patrols the skies.

?DID YOU KNOW? Some of *T. REX*'S RELATIVES APPARENTLY WERE FEATHERED. What about the giant dino itself? Scientists aren't sure yet, but it's possible. SO FAR, THE PATCHY FOSSILS OF *T. REX* SKIN THEY'VE FOUND HAVE BEEN SCALY.

1 Long, slender hind legs, long necks, and small heads are the marks of **ornithomimids (meaning "bird mimics")**, ostrichlike dinosaurs from the late Cretaceous period.

2 Ornithomimid brain cavities are relatively big, so the birdlike dinosaurs may have had large brains. They could have been fairly smart.

3 Ornithomimids weren't the biggest dinosaurs, but they **may have been the fastest.** They could have run as fast as a racehorse as they chased down their prey.

4 Ornithomimid feet had sharp claws that gripped the ground as they ran.

5 The first ornithomimid was discovered by the famous paleontologist Othniel Charles Marsh in 1889 in Colorado, U.S.A. He named it *Ornithomimus velox*, or "speedy bird mimic."

6 Ornithomimids lived in North America, Asia, Europe, and Australia. They might have thrived in so many different places because they could eat a wide variety of foods with their beaklike jaws, including plants, small mammals, and insects.

7 *Archaeornithomimus* ("ancient bird mimic"), from China, was 11 feet (3 m) long but weighed only as much as a 12-year-old girl. It may have had a **coat of feathers**.

ABOUT ORNITHOMIMIDS

8 *Gallimimus*'s name means "chicken mimic," but this ornithomimid was not chicken-size. *Gallimimus* was 20 feet (6 m) long— longer than a pickup truck—and weighed 440 pounds (200 kg).

9 *Gallimimus* is one of the dinosaur stars of the movie *Jurassic Park*. The movie shows them running away from a *T. rex*. Scientists don't actually know if these animals ran in groups.

10 *Struthiomimus* was 14 feet (4 m) long. Its tail made up much of that length. This fast-moving dino may have held its tail out stiff behind it to balance while running.

11 *Deinocheirus mirificus* (meaning "terrible hands that look peculiar") was named for its eight-foot (2.4-m) arms and eight-inch (20-cm)-long giant claws.

12 In 2009, paleontologists found another *Deinocheirus* fossil that turned out to be a huge, heavy ornithomimid, almost as big as a *T. rex*.

13 In 1981, scientists in Mongolia found one of the earliest ornithomimids, the small, short-armed *Harpymimus*. Unlike later ornithomimids, it had a few blunt teeth in its jaws.

14 Paleontologists found the fossils of a herd of young *Sinornithomimus* dinos that all died at once near a lake in Mongolia. The unlucky creatures might have gotten stuck in the mud.

15 *Ornithomimus* survived right up to the big extinction that wiped out dinosaurs about 65 million years ago.

Ostrich-like *Struthiomimus*, perhaps the fastest dinosaur

73

1 **Dromaeosaurs** were a group of **fierce, two-legged meat-eaters** that stalked their prey during the Cretaceous period. They are popularly known as raptors, meaning they took their prey by force.

2 Dromaeosaur arms and hands were specialized for killing. Their flexible wrists and sharp claws allowed them to easily grab and hold on to their prey.

3 **Dromaeosaurs had a killing claw on their second toe** that could sweep down and rip into a victim.

4 Paleontologist John Ostrom studied the big-clawed dromaeosaur *Deinonychus* in the 1960s. His research showed dinosaurs were **not all slow and sluggish**—some were fast and even graceful.

5 *Utahraptor* would have been one scary dinosaur. The biggest of the dromaeosaurs, it grew up to 20 feet (6 m) long. Its powerful legs had thick, nine-inch (23-cm) killing claws.

6 A nine-ton (8.2-t) sandstone block uncovered in Utah, U.S.A., held the remains of at least six *Utahraptors*. The find may show that the big predators hunted in packs.

7 *Deinonychus* fossils are often found with the fossils of *Tenontosaurus*, plant-eating dinosaurs. **The *Deinonychus* raptors may have hunted in groups for young tenontosaurs.**

RAPTORS

8 *Conchoraptor* had a powerful beak, which it may have used to crack open snails or other shelled creatures.

9 Quill knob marks on a Mongolian *Velociraptor*'s forearm show that the fierce creature was covered in feathers.

10 The *Velociraptors* shown in the *Jurassic Park* movies are human-size, but real *Velociraptors* were about the size of big dogs.

11 Studies of *Bambiraptor* skulls suggest that the long-legged little raptors had a good sense of smell, similar to that of today's vultures.

12 Most meat-eating raptors had teeth, but not all. Big, birdlike *Oviraptor* had a beak, possibly for eating eggs or shellfish.

13 Covered with feathers, *Microraptor* was the smallest dromaeosaur yet discovered. This Chinese raptor was between one and three feet (0.3 and 0.9 m) long.

14 Claw fossils and a pelvis fossil found in Canada's Alberta Province in 1982 belonged to the tiniest dromaeosaur yet found in North America. Smaller than a chicken, *Hesperonychus* probably hunted little mammals, insects, or amphibians.

15 Dromaeosaurs were probably scavengers as well as predators. The fossil of a *Velociraptor* was found with a bone in its gut from a flying pterosaur, which it likely didn't kill itself.

A pack of *Deinonychus* feasts on a big plant-eating *Tenontosaurus*.

1 From prehistoric times sharks have **constantly grown new teeth and dropped old ones,** which have turned into fossils.

2 Some **Paleozoic limestone rocks are filled** with hundreds of tiny, sharp microteeth, called **conodonts,** left behind by early jawless fish.

3 The huge sharklike fish *Edestus,* known only from jaw fossils, had **one straight line of teeth** on its top and bottom jaws, like a pair of scissors.

4 **Dromaeosaur (raptor) claws were covered by keratin,** the same hard substance that makes up your fingernails.

5 The fossil of a stocky, **birdlike predator** found in Romania had two big, sharp claws on each foot. Scientists think the dinosaur, named *Balaur bondoc* ("stocky dragon"), might have held down its prey with these claws.

6 Recent **shark teeth are white, but fossil teeth** darken over time, turning gray or black.

7 A small jaw fossil found in Australia in 2016 came from the squirrel-size mammal known as a **marsupial lion** because it chased down prey like a lion does. Its name: *Microleo.*

CLAWS AND JAWS

8 Paleontologists can **calculate the strength of a fossil jaw by scanning** it with a laser and then testing a model of it on a computer.

9 **The chemical makeup of fossil teeth** can tell paleontologists a lot about the climate—the temperature and moisture—in which an animal lived.

10 An expedition to Mongolia in 1948 found the biggest claw fossils ever discovered. The 3.3-foot (1-m)-long claws turned out to be part of *Therizinosaurus,* a **large theropod plant-eater** with eight-foot (2.4-m)-long arms.

11 The long jaws of "SuperCroc" *Sarcosuchus* had 100 teeth and could bite down with the weight of a heavy truck.

12 **The claws on some raptors' feet were retractable,** like a cat's claws. They could be pulled up off the ground and back toward the foot.

13 A crocodile jaw fossil found on an island near Africa's Madagascar matched the tooth marks on a tortoiseshell fossil there, showing that either the crocs attacked living tortoises or scavenged on dead ones.

14 Most of the bony fish called **pycnodontiforms had flat teeth** for crushing and chewing, but a new fossil found in Germany had pointy, piranha-like teeth instead. Like modern piranhas, *Piranhamesodon pinnatomus* might have chomped on the fins of its fellow swimmers.

15 An amateur fossil hunter on a beach in Australia thought at first he had dug up an old World War II weapon, but in fact he had found **a foot-long fossilized tooth** from an extinct sperm whale.

Therizinosaurus in a forest at dusk

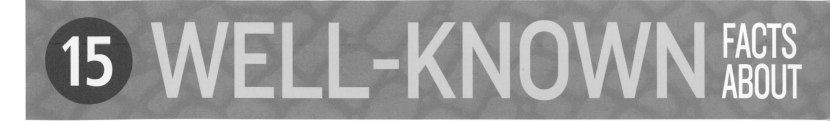

1 Discovered in 1861 in Germany's Solnhofen limestone, the beautiful fossil of *Archaeopteryx lithographica* filled in a missing link between dinosaurs and birds. It is now held in Berlin's Natural History Museum.

2 The worker who dug up the famous *Archaeopteryx* fossil traded it to a local doctor to pay his medical bill.

3 Discovered in Mongolia in 1971, the Fighting Dinosaurs fossil captures the moment when a *Velociraptor* sank its claws into the neck of a *Protoceratops*—while the *Protoceratops* was biting into the *Velociraptor*'s arm. The fossil is a **Mongolian national treasure.**

4 The immense skeleton of a *Diplodocus carnegii* sauropod was **transported in 130 separate crates** from Wyoming to the Carnegie Museum of Natural History in Pittsburgh, Pennsylvania, U.S.A.

5 Discovered in China's Liaoning Province, a detailed fossil of *Sinosauropteryx* was the first fossil to show that some dinosaurs had feathers. The main specimen of the fossil, **nicknamed "Dave,"** is held in the Geological Museum of China.

6 The fossilized jaw of **Megalosaurus,** the **first dinosaur fossil** to be described by scientists in 1824, can still be seen in the Oxford University Museum of Natural History.

7 In 1990, in South Dakota, U.S.A., fossil collector Sue Hendrickson found the biggest and most complete *Tyrannosaurus rex* skeleton ever. The reassembled skeleton, also known as Sue, now resides at Chicago's Field Museum.

FAMOUS FOSSILS

Sue, the biggest, most complete *Tyrannosaurus rex* ever found

8 Sue the *T. rex* fossil has its own Twitter account.

9 Discovered near a village in India, a rare fossil shows an 11.5-foot (3.5-m)-long snake, *Sanajeh indicus,* about to eat a titanosaur hatchling.

10 The fossil of a skeleton with eggs discovered in Mongolia turned out to be an adult *Oviraptor* curled around a nest with 20 eggs. The fossil is nicknamed "Brooding Mama." The original was returned to Mongolia, but a cast can be seen at the American Museum of Natural History in New York City.

11 The beautifully preserved Ichthyosaur skeleton discovered by fossil hunter Mary Anning in 1811 can still be seen in London's Natural History Museum.

12 First spotted in Australia in 1947, leaflike *Dickinsonia* fossils—almost 600 million years old—are among the most ancient animals ever found. Specimens can be seen at the South Australian Museum in Adelaide.

13 Discovered standing up in a bog, the famous "Warren mastodon" skeleton in New York City's American Museum of Natural History has 8.5-foot (2.6-m)-long tusks.

14 Many of the bizarre creatures fossilized in Canada's Burgess shale, including *Hallucigenia,* were sent to Washington, D.C.'s Smithsonian Institution. They can be seen in the National Museum of Natural History.

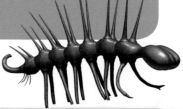

15 Many human ancestor fossils are famous, especially "Lucy," a partial *Australopithecus* skeleton discovered in Ethiopia. The original is in a safe in Ethiopia, but a cast can be seen at the Cleveland Museum of Natural History in Ohio, U.S.A.

79

1 WESTERN NORTH AMERICA was underwater in prehistoric times, which preserved animal remains. The land then rose into mountains, exposing fossils.

2 Much of the land in the West is dry, without many trees or shrubs. THIS MAKES IT EASIER TO SPOT FOSSILS IN THE GROUND.

3 The Green River formation, which includes FOSSIL BUTTE NATIONAL MONUMENT in Wyoming, is rich with plant and animal fossils.

4 The HELL CREEK FORMATION of Montana, is in North America's badlands—a rocky area perfect for finding exposed fossils.

5 One of the most complete *T. rex* skeletons, the "WANKEL REX," was found at Montana's Hell Creek formation by a fossil hunter in 1988.

6 HELL CREEK IS FULL OF *TRICERATOPS* FOSSILS, including more than 50 skulls and at least one complete skeleton.

7 The TWO MEDICINE FORMATION in Montana has some 200 specimens of *Maiasaura*, the "good mother" dinosaur, with hatchlings and eggs.

8 New Mexico's Ghost Ranch is known for its *COELOPHYSIS* FOSSILS. The slender dinosaur is now the state fossil of New Mexico.

9 Arizona's Grand Canyon rocks hold many ancient fossils, including STROMATOLITES, PRIMITIVE BACTERIA more than a billion years old.

10 Colorado's FLORISSANT FOSSIL BEDS holds a perfectly preserved *Prodryas persephone* butterfly, with clear patterns on its wings.

11 On the Colorado-Utah border, the rocks in DINOSAUR NATIONAL MONUMENT contain thousands of Jurassic-age fossils.

12 Formations at Dinosaur National Monument hold SAUROPODS, LONG-NECKED PLANT-EATING DINOSAURS, with some complete skulls.

13 More than 1,500 dinosaur fossils are visible in the cliff face at DINOSAUR NATIONAL MONUMENT'S EXHIBIT HALL.

14 In Texas, the PALUXY RIVER BEDS contain excellent dinosaur tracks. Untrue stories once said that human footprints were found beside them.

15 UTAH'S WHEELER SHALE contains so many trilobite fossils that some are sold as belt buckles, earrings, and tie clasps.

35 FACTS ABOUT FOSSIL HOT SPOTS:

Echo Park in Dinosaur National Monument

16 ARIZONA'S PETRIFIED FOREST NATIONAL PARK has colorful *Araucarioxylon arizonicum* tree trunks, known as rainbow wood.

17 The Petrified Forest National Park is also famous for fossils of reptiles, such as the CROCODILE-LIKE PHYTOSAURS.

18 Texas's WACO MAMMOTH NATIONAL MONUMENT contains rare fossils of 19 adult and young Columbian mammoths, apparently drowned in flash floods.

19 The town of Barstow in California's Mojave Desert has fossil TRACKS OF CAMELS, PYGMY RHINOS, AND SABER-TOOTHED CATS.

20 The LA BREA TAR PITS in Los Angeles trapped thousands of Ice Age mammals in sticky natural asphalt seeping from the ground.

21 Glacier National Park in Montana has billion-year-old STROMATOLITES and younger fossils, like 34-million-year-old early horses.

22 Oregon's JOHN DAY FOSSIL BEDS hold relatively recent fossils of ancient fruits, and mammals such as the rhino-like brontothere.

23 Fish fans can see perfectly preserved imprints of sharks, coelacanths, and sea stars at the BEAR GULCH LIMESTONE in Montana.

24 A skeleton of a crocodile relative was found on the ranch of the painter GEORGIA O'KEEFFE. The creature was named *Effigia okeeffeae*, for her.

25 Walk where dinosaurs once trod at DINOSAUR RIDGE, near Morrison, Colorado. Three-toed tracks of ornithopods are clearly visible there.

26 *STEGOSAURUS* and *ALLOSAURUS* fossils were found at Colorado's Morrison formation, which includes Dinosaur Ridge.

27 The CLEVELAND-LLOYD DINOSAUR QUARRY in Utah is a hotbed of allosaur bones and holds 11 other species, including *Camarasaurus*.

28 An ancient lake bed near Clarkia, Idaho, is now the CLARKIA FOSSIL BEDS. They hold rare, perfectly preserved leaf and fish fossils.

29 In the badlands of Alberta Province in Canada, DINOSAUR PROVINCIAL PARK has yielded more than 500 Cretaceous species.

30 Found in Dinosaur Provincial Park, *CHASMOSAURUS BELLI* is a plant-eating dinosaur whose skull has a huge bony frill with two oval holes.

31 *CHASMOSAURUS* inspired two Pokémon Fossil characters, SHIELDON and BASTIODON, who wear helmets for butting heads.

32 A 68-million-year-old *T. rex* called "SCOTTY" is the OFFICIAL FOSSIL OF THE PROVINCE OF SASKATCHEWAN.

33 Glen Guthrie—the cook for a 2001 paleontology expedition in Alberta—found the first known *EOTRICERATOPS*, a relative of *Triceratops*.

34 The famous fossil of *TIKTAALIK*, a link between fish and four-legged animals, was named for a local fish by Inuit elders of Canada's Nunavut territory.

35 The LARGEST MOSASAUR SKELETON on display, 42.7 feet (13 m) long, is in the Canadian Fossil Discovery Centre and is nicknamed "BRUCE."

WESTERN NORTH AMERICA

1 Most dinosaurs became **EXTINCT ABOUT 65 MILLION YEARS AGO,** but the branch of their relatives that includes early birds lived on to evolve into today's birds.

2 In the **CRETACEOUS-PALEOGENE MASS EXTINCTION,** ground-living ancestors of birds survived, but tree dwellers died off. This might mean that wildfires from an asteroid impact wiped out forests and the animals in their trees.

3 *ARCHAEOPTERYX* fossils, first discovered in 1860, had **FEATHERS, BUT ALSO TEETH, WING CLAWS,** and a bony tail. Scientists eventually realized the animal was a link between dinosaurs and birds.

4 Only 11 good *ARCHAEOPTERYX* fossils have been discovered, and one vanished—possibly stolen—after its owner died in 1991.

5 **SKELETONS OF THEROPOD DINOSAURS** and those of modern birds have many of the same features in their hands (wings), backbones, and skulls.

25 FLYING FACTS ABOUT

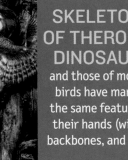

6 Most scientists think **PTEROSAURS—FLYING REPTILES—**did not have feathers. However, some pterosaur fossils have marks that might show some kind of downy featherlike covering.

7 *OVIRAPTOR* **FOSSILS,** found hunched over eggs, have long arm feathers. The feathers might have helped to keep the eggs warm.

8 The only known fossil of *EPIDEXIPTERYX,* a little Jurassic dinosaur found in Mongolia, has FOUR LONG TAIL FEATHERS that might have helped it attract mates.

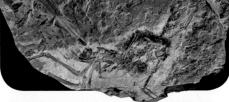

9 *MICRORAPTOR,* found in China, is the only creature discovered so far with four wings.

10 In spite of its four wings, *MICRORAPTOR* probably couldn't fly well. It may have been able to glide from tree to tree.

11 In a marketplace in Myanmar, a scientist found a piece of amber holding a perfectly preserved tail of a **FEATHERED BABY DINOSAUR.**

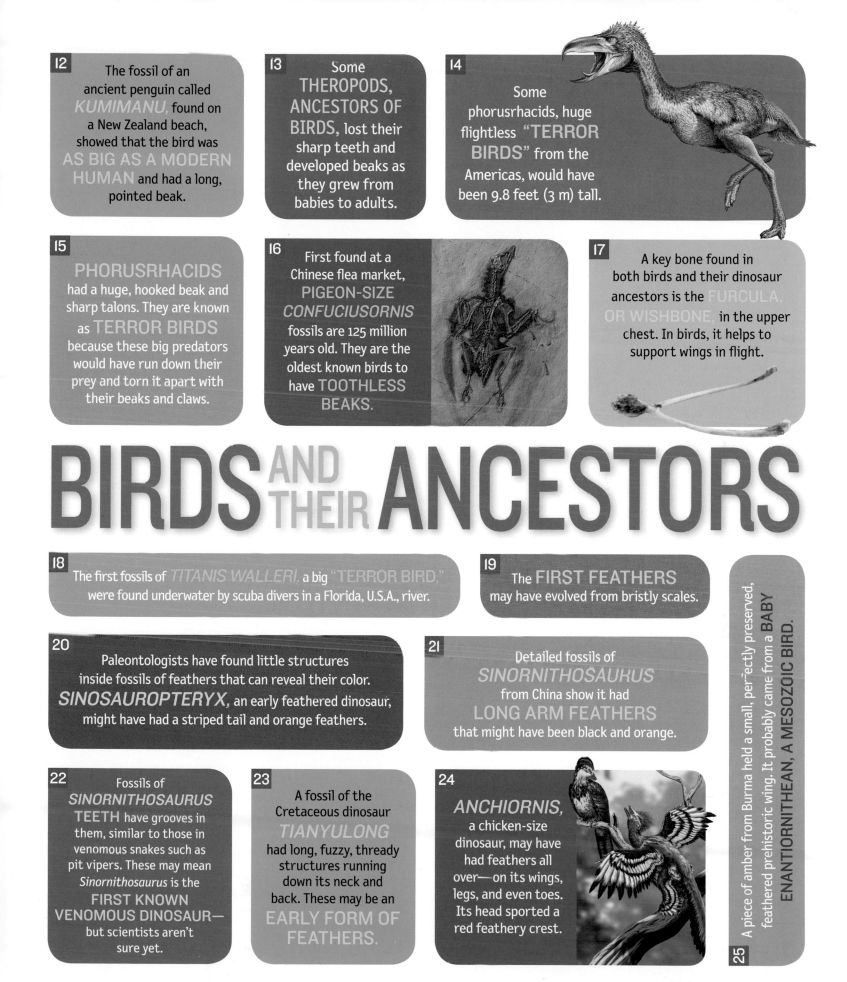

12 The fossil of an ancient penguin called *KUMIMANU,* found on a New Zealand beach, showed that the bird was AS BIG AS A MODERN HUMAN and had a long, pointed beak.

13 Some THEROPODS, ANCESTORS OF BIRDS, lost their sharp teeth and developed beaks as they grew from babies to adults.

14 Some phorusrhacids, huge flightless "TERROR BIRDS" from the Americas, would have been 9.8 feet (3 m) tall.

15 PHORUSRHACIDS had a huge, hooked beak and sharp talons. They are known as TERROR BIRDS because these big predators would have run down their prey and torn it apart with their beaks and claws.

16 First found at a Chinese flea market, PIGEON-SIZE *CONFUCIUSORNIS* fossils are 125 million years old. They are the oldest known birds to have TOOTHLESS BEAKS.

17 A key bone found in both birds and their dinosaur ancestors is the FURCULA, OR WISHBONE, in the upper chest. In birds, it helps to support wings in flight.

BIRDS AND THEIR ANCESTORS

18 The first fossils of *TITANIS WALLERI,* a big "TERROR BIRD," were found underwater by scuba divers in a Florida, U.S.A., river.

19 The FIRST FEATHERS may have evolved from bristly scales.

20 Paleontologists have found little structures inside fossils of feathers that can reveal their color. *SINOSAUROPTERYX,* an early feathered dinosaur, might have had a striped tail and orange feathers.

21 Detailed fossils of *SINORNITHOSAURUS* from China show it had LONG ARM FEATHERS that might have been black and orange.

22 Fossils of *SINORNITHOSAURUS* TEETH have grooves in them, similar to those in venomous snakes such as pit vipers. These may mean *Sinornithosaurus* is the FIRST KNOWN VENOMOUS DINOSAUR— but scientists aren't sure yet.

23 A fossil of the Cretaceous dinosaur *TIANYULONG* had long, fuzzy, thready structures running down its neck and back. These may be an EARLY FORM OF FEATHERS.

24 *ANCHIORNIS,* a chicken-size dinosaur, may have had feathers all over—on its wings, legs, and even toes. Its head sported a red feathery crest.

25 A piece of amber from Burma held a small, perfectly preserved, feathered prehistoric wing. It probably came from a BABY ENANTIORNITHEAN, A MESOZOIC BIRD.

15 FAULTY FACTS

❶ In 1845, fossil collector Albert Koch mistakenly added a lot of bones to the skeleton of the early whale *Basilosaurus,* and determined it was a "sea serpent."

❷ The fossil of the scaly Carboniferous tree *Lepidodendron* was displayed in Wales in 1851 as a serpent.

❸ Old illustrations used to show big *Brachiosaurus,* with its nostrils on top of its skull, living in the water. We now know that *Brachiosaurus* lived on land.

❹ *Oviraptor* got its name—which means "egg thief"—because the first good fossil was found next to what were thought to be *Protoceratops* eggs. Later, paleontologists realized that these were its own eggs.

❺ In the 1920s, the paleontologist who put together a *Megalosaurus* skeleton added in the sail-backed spine of a spinosaur.

❻ Paleontologist Gideon Mantell displayed one of the first dinosaurs ever discovered, *Iguanodon,* with a spike on its nose. That spike was actually part of its thumb.

❼ Nineteenth-century paleontologist Othniel Charles Marsh examined the skull of a *Triceratops* and declared that it was an extinct bison.

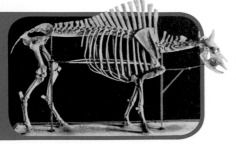

Brachiosaurus in a swamp

ABOUT FOSSIL MISTAKES

8 When paleontologist Richard Owen first wrote about the famous *Archaeopteryx* fossil in Germany, he described it upside down.

9 In 1922, paleontologist Dr. Henry Osborn identified a tooth found in Nebraska, U.S.A., as belonging to an apelike human ancestor, soon nicknamed **"Nebraska Man."** The tooth turned out to belong to a peccary, **a hoglike animal.**

10 Known as **Brontosaurus,** the big sauropod skeleton shown at the American Museum of Natural History in 1905 was actually an **Apatosaurus** body with a **Camarasaurus** head.

11 The paleontologist who first discovered the long-clawed theropod dinosaur ***Therizinosaurus*** thought it was a big turtlelike reptile that ate seaweed.

12 In 1725, Johann Scheuchzer named a fossilized skeleton *Homo diluvii testis,* roughly translated as "a human victim of Noah's flood." It turned out to be a giant salamander.

13 Paleontologists now think that *Stygimoloch spinifer,* a thick-skulled dinosaur named as a new species in 1973, is just a young pachycephalosaur.

14 Early models of *Tyrannosaurus rex* stood mostly upright with its tail dragging on the ground. We now know that this would have fractured some of its bones. *T. rex* ran with its tail sticking out behind it.

15 New species are often given wrong scientific names. For instance, different-looking fossils might be given different scientific names, then later prove to be the same species.

1 China has yielded some of the **best fossil discoveries** in the last 100 years, including a wealth of dinosaurs and ancestors of birds.

2 China's Lufeng rocks, in the southern part of the country, contain early Jurassic dinosaurs, including a number of **long-necked sauropods.**

3 Many specimens of *Lufengosaurus,* a midsize prosauropod (a sauropod ancestor), have been discovered in China's Lufeng County. This plant-eating dinosaur could rise up on its heavy hind legs to strip leaves from trees.

4 *Incisivosaurus,* a relative of *Oviraptor*, looked like a cartoon creature. The **chicken-size theropod** had feathers, huge claws, and a beak—with big buck teeth sticking out of it.

5 The Jehol fossil beds in northeast China are rich in well-preserved early Cretaceous creatures. They include mammals, birds, insects, pterosaurs, and dinosaurs—**including spectacular feathered dinosaurs.**

6 Unlike most places on Earth, Mongolia's Gobi has almost the same habitat today as it did in prehistoric times—a desert environment. Many fossils can be found in its sands.

7 The big Chinese sauropod *Shunosaurus* had a football-shaped club on the end of its tail, which it might have swung to protect itself from enemies.

A model of feathered *Caudipteryx zoui*

8 China's *Beipiaosaurus* was a seven-foot (2.1-m)-tall therizinosaur (a two-legged, big-clawed theropod). It was covered by a combination of **small downy feathers** and long feathers.

9 *Sinornis, a small early bird,* had traits of both birds and earlier dinosaurs. Like *Archaeopteryx*, it had a beak with teeth, but it was better adapted for flight.

10 Fossils of **turkey-size** *Caudipteryx* preserved beautiful impressions of long feathers on its front arms. The little theropod would not have been able to fly, which might mean that feathers first evolved for reasons other than flight.

11 Farmers in China found the fossil of what might be the **first gliding mammal.** The squirrel-size creature, *Volaticotherium,* had membranes that stretched between its front and hind limbs.

12 *Caihong juji,* **a birdlike dinosaur** found in China, had shimmering feathers that might have given off rainbowlike colors.

13 *Repenomamus,* **a badgerlike mammal** from the Cretaceous, was found in northeastern China. It had a baby dinosaur in its stomach.

14 China's *Liaoceratops* was an early relative of *Triceratops*. It had a modest frill and was only the **size of a dog.**

15 Fossils of *Yutyrannus,* a 30-foot (9-m) tyrannosaur found in China, **had feathers up to eight inches** (20 cm) long.

❶ All dinosaurs hatched from eggs, like today's reptiles and birds.

❷ Most egg fossils aren't shaped like chicken eggs. They range from round balls to long, slender torpedo shapes.

❸ How can you tell an egg fossil from an egg-shaped rock? Egg fossils are typically cracked and thin, with a fine pattern across their surfaces.

❹ Scans of beautifully preserved dinosaur eggs found in a fossilized Montana, U.S.A., nest revealed baby *Troodons* inside.

❺ Scientists studying fossilized dinosaur nests believe that some dinosaurs sat in a hollow space in the middle of the nest, so they could keep eggs warm without crushing them.

❻ Researchers believe that **dinosaur eggs came in many colors,** some with speckles, like bird eggs today.

❼ A paleontologist discovered two dinosaur eggs with visible embryos next to a road cut out of the landscape in South Africa. The embryos turned out to belong to *Massospondylus,* a small sauropod.

DINOSAUR BABIES

Titanosaurus watches over its eggs and babies.

8 Scientists studying growth lines in *Protoceratops* embryos found that it would have taken **three to six months for them to hatch from an egg**—much longer than it takes for baby birds to hatch.

9 Some dinosaurs **laid their eggs in a neat spiral.**

10 Auca Mahuevo, in Argentina, is one of the **world's great dinosaur nesting grounds.** There, female titanosaurs dug out shallow nests and laid thousands of eggs.

11 Babies of *Massospondylus* didn't look or move like the grown-ups. Instead of a long neck and a two-legged walking style, the babies had a **short neck and walked on all fours.**

12 On average, **baby sauropods weighed about 11 pounds (5 kg) at birth.** By the time they were adults, they weighed 10,000 times as much.

13 *Stegosaurus* tracks found in Colorado, U.S.A., show that adult stegosaurs traveled alongside their **seven-pound (3-kg) babies.**

14 **Baby dinosaurs needed to grow fast** and become independent to escape predators. Most nestlings probably didn't survive to adulthood.

15 Because young dinosaurs can look very different from adults, **paleontologists sometimes mistakenly think they belong to different species.**

THERE'S A LOT WE DON'T KNOW YET ABOUT DINOSAUR PARENTING. Scientists base their ideas about dinosaur families partly on studies of modern-day birds and crocodiles. For instance, **PLANT FOSSILS FOUND NEAR NESTS MIGHT HAVE BEEN THE REMAINS OF FOOD THAT PARENTS CHEWED UP TO FEED THEIR YOUNG,** much as birds do. New discoveries every year are helping to fill in the dinosaur family picture.

DID YOU KNOW?

90

DINOSAUR FAMILIES

In 1978, Marion Brandvold, who owned a rock store in Bynum, Montana, U.S.A., took paleontologist Jack Horner to a rocky site outside of Choteau, Montana, where she had found the bones of young dinosaurs. The area turned out to hold more than just bones. It also contained the fossilized remains of 14 egg-filled dinosaur nests. The nests belonged to a new kind of hadrosaur, or duck-billed dinosaur, that Horner went on to name *Maiasaura*, "good mother lizard." The way the nests were arranged, and the tiny and fairly helpless state of the newborn babies, implied that the maiasaurs stayed with the babies, fed them, and protected them.

Since that time, other dinosaurs, such as *Oviraptor* and *Troodon*, have also been found with their nests. Some baby dinosaurs would not have been able to move around much at birth, so their parents probably took care of them for a while. Others were well developed when they hatched, and might have been independent almost right away. Baby dinosaurs started off quite small and grew fast, changing their size much more drastically than today's animals. Trackways and fossils of young and adult dinosaurs together show that at least some dinosaur families stayed and traveled together.

A parent *Mussaurus* watches over its nest.

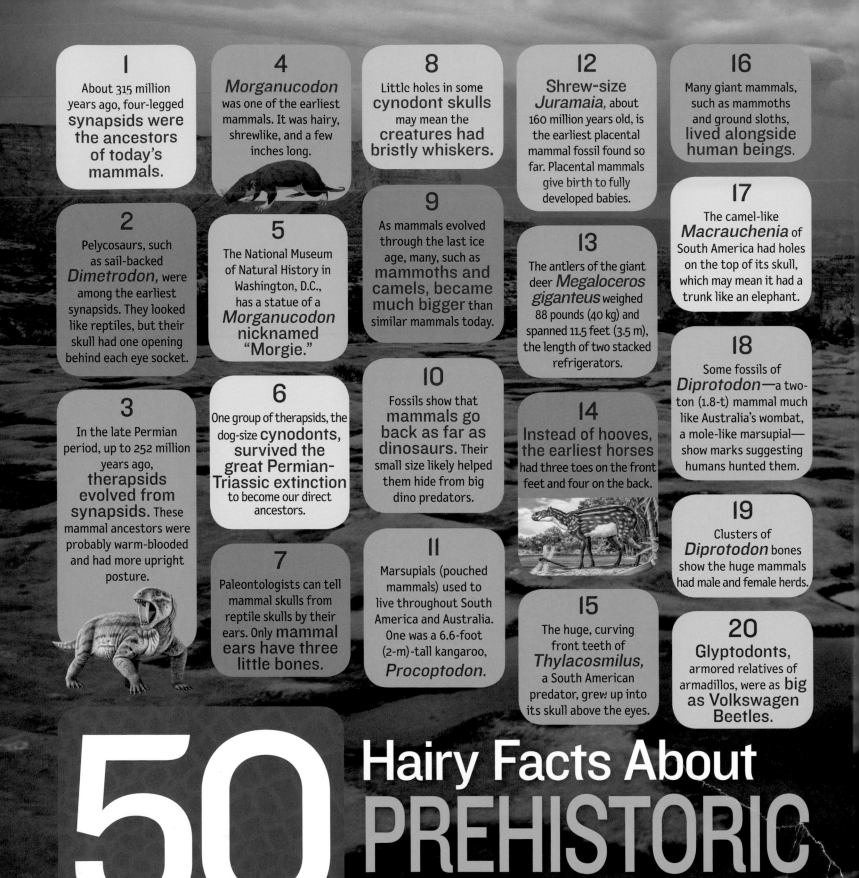

1
About 315 million years ago, four-legged **synapsids were the ancestors of today's mammals.**

4
Morganucodon was one of the earliest mammals. It was hairy, shrewlike, and a few inches long.

8
Little holes in some **cynodont skulls** may mean the **creatures had bristly whiskers.**

12
Shrew-size *Juramaia,* about 160 million years old, is the earliest placental mammal fossil found so far. Placental mammals give birth to fully developed babies.

16
Many giant mammals, such as mammoths and ground sloths, **lived alongside human beings.**

2
Pelycosaurs, such as sail-backed *Dimetrodon,* were among the earliest synapsids. They looked like reptiles, but their skull had one opening behind each eye socket.

5
The National Museum of Natural History in Washington, D.C., has a statue of a *Morganucodon* nicknamed "Morgie."

9
As mammals evolved through the last ice age, many, such as **mammoths and camels, became much bigger** than similar mammals today.

13
The antlers of the giant deer *Megaloceros giganteus* weighed 88 pounds (40 kg) and spanned 11.5 feet (3.5 m), the length of two stacked refrigerators.

17
The camel-like *Macrauchenia* of South America had holes on the top of its skull, which may mean it had a trunk like an elephant.

3
In the late Permian period, up to 252 million years ago, **therapsids evolved from synapsids.** These mammal ancestors were probably warm-blooded and had more upright posture.

6
One group of therapsids, the dog-size **cynodonts, survived the great Permian-Triassic extinction** to become our direct ancestors.

10
Fossils show that **mammals go back as far as dinosaurs.** Their small size likely helped them hide from big dino predators.

14
Instead of hooves, the earliest horses had three toes on the front feet and four on the back.

18
Some fossils of *Diprotodon*—a two-ton (1.8-t) mammal much like Australia's wombat, a mole-like marsupial—show marks suggesting humans hunted them.

7
Paleontologists can tell mammal skulls from reptile skulls by their ears. Only **mammal ears have three little bones.**

11
Marsupials (pouched mammals) used to live throughout South America and Australia. One was a 6.6-foot (2-m)-tall kangaroo, *Procoptodon.*

15
The huge, curving front teeth of *Thylacosmilus,* a South American predator, grew up into its skull above the eyes.

19
Clusters of *Diprotodon* bones show the huge mammals had male and female herds.

20
Glyptodonts, armored relatives of armadillos, were as big as Volkswagen Beetles.

50 Hairy Facts About PREHISTORIC LAND MAMMALS

A prehistoric landscape

21
Huge rodent *Josephoartigasia monesi* bit down with three times a tiger's force.

22
Little mammals sometimes chewed on big dinosaurs. Rodent-like bite marks have been found on dino fossils in Canada.

23
Giraffe-like *Xenokeryx amidalae* had a T-shaped horn and is named for the Star Wars character Padmé Amidala.

24
Fossil skulls of *Arsinoitherium*, a rhinolike mammal from North Africa, had two gigantic horns five feet (1.5 m) long.

25
In Wyoming, U.S.A., bite marks on the bones of camel-like *Poebrotherium* match the jaws of the hippo relative *Archaeotherium.*

26
Megatherium americanum, a giant ground sloth, stood 12 feet (3.7 m) tall on its hind feet.

27
The first fossil of *Megatherium* was discovered on a riverbank in Argentina in 1788.

28
An early expert thought that *Megatherium* used its huge claws to burrow through the ground. Likely it used them to pull down branches for food.

29
Tool marks on fossils of Jefferson ground sloth bones show that early **North American humans feasted on sloth.**

30
People exploring a volcanic hole in New Mexico, U.S.A., found a complete **mummified Shasta ground sloth** buried in bat poop.

31
A scientist in New Mexico found human **footprints inside giant sloth footprints**. The human might have been tracking the sloth.

32
Palaeocastor, a prehistoric beaver from North America, dug long spiral burrows into the ground. The geologists who found the burrows called them devil's corkscrews.

33
Venezuela's *Phoberomys pattersoni* resembled an enormous guinea pig—as long as today's tigers.

34
The front legs of *Chalicotherium*, a horselike mammal, were longer than its hind legs. It walked on its knuckles like a gorilla.

35
Bear-dogs, related to dogs today, were **predators** in Europe, North America, and Africa. They weighed as much as today's lions.

36
In North America's Mojave Desert there are tracks of a **bear-dog chasing a pronghorn**—a fast, deerlike animal—20 million years ago.

37
The first true dogs evolved in North America 40 million years ago. The jaws of bear-size *Epicyon* could crush bone.

38
Dire wolves (*Canis dirus*), bigger than today's gray wolves, hunted in packs in Ice Age North America.

39
Dire wolves were common in California, U.S.A. The La Brea Tar Pits exhibit some 400 dire wolf skulls.

40
The fossil record shows that some **mammals isolated on islands evolved to be smaller** than their mainland relatives.

41
Uintatheres, rhino-size plant-eaters, had knobby skulls with huge canine teeth sticking down from their upper jaws.

42
The early bat *Onychonycteris finneyi* had well-developed wings but lacked the sensitive inner ears that today's bats use to capture sound to help them navigate.

43
Researchers at the **La Brea Tar Pits** have excavated several jawbones of saber-toothed kittens.

44
Pseudaelurus, a short-legged cat a bit larger than today's house cats, was the first true cat in North America. It entered from Asia over the Bering Land Bridge.

45
Smilodon, the saber-toothed cat, had huge canine teeth. In the biggest species, *Smilodon populator,* they were as long as a butcher knife.

46
Even though it had huge teeth, *Smilodon* had a weak bite. It might have used its strong neck and legs to hold prey while it slashed with its canines.

47
Smilodon is California's state fossil.

48
Camelops, a big prehistoric camel, first evolved in North America. After millions of years, it became extinct about 11,000 years ago.

49
Paraceratherium was one of the biggest land animals ever to walk on Earth. This long-necked, rhinolike plant-eater was bigger and heavier than today's elephants.

50
Eosimias ("dawn monkey") was a distant human relative and one of the earliest primates ever discovered. Living in Chinese forests 40 million years ago, it weighed as much as a hamster.

1 Seven kinds of ocean mammals, including **WHALES, MANATEES, AND SEALS, STARTED OFF AS LAND ANIMALS** that evolved into sea creatures.

2 **THE OLDEST FOSSILS OF WHALE ANCESTORS** were found in 40- to 50-million-year-old rocks.

3 **WHALES AND DOLPHINS EVOLVED FROM** the same prehistoric ancestors as **HIPPOS**.

4 Fossils found in Pakistan in the 1980s turned out to be an **EARLY WHALE ANCESTOR,** *PAKICETUS*. It was a wolf-size, sharp-snouted mammal that lived near rivers.

5 *PAKICETUS* probably **WALKED MOSTLY ON LAND,** while sometimes wading through the water.

25 DEEP-DIVING FACTS ABOUT

6 It took about **12 MILLION YEARS** for whale ancestors to go from living on land to living completely in the sea.

7 As whales evolved in the water, their legs grew shorter and shorter, and their **FRONT LEGS EVOLVED INTO FLIPPERS.**

8 Fossils of *RODHOCETUS,* A HIPPOLIKE ANCESTOR OF WHALES, show it had a streamlined body for swimming, but it still had hooves at the ends of its front limbs.

9 With short legs, a powerful tail, and a long, skinny jaw, *REMINGTONOCETUS* was a **WHALE ANCESTOR** that may have looked like an otter with a pointy beak.

10 Early whale *BASILOSAURUS* had tiny hind feet, about five inches (13 cm) long. It wasn't big enough to hold up its weight on land.

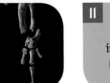

11 *BASILOSAURUS* is the state fossil of Alabama, U.S.A., and Mississippi, U.S.A.

12 Wadi Al-Hitan, in Egypt's western deserts, is known as **VALLEY OF THE WHALES** because it holds hundreds of early whale fossils in its rocks.

13 One of the driest places on Earth holds a wealth of marine fossils. **CERRO BALLENA,** in Chile's Atacama Desert, has about **40 FOSSILS** of **WHALES** as well as seals and aquatic sloths.

14 The Cerro Ballena mammals might have **DIED FROM POISONOUS ALGAE,** tiny plants that can release toxins into the water.

15 Discovered in Pakistan in the 1990s, a nearly complete skeleton turned out to be a crocodile-like whale ancestor that lived in water but may have been able to waddle on land with its four squat legs. It was named **AMBULOCETUS,** "walking whale."

16 Like modern-day crocodiles, *AMBULOCETUS* may have **LURKED IN THE WATER** near the shore and **THEN LUNGED OUT TO GRAB ITS PREY.**

17 *MAIACETUS,* a 40-million-year-old whale ancestor, was a streamlined mammal that spent much of its time in water, but **GAVE BIRTH ON LAND.**

OCEAN MAMMALS

18 Early whales, such as 40-million-year-old *DORUDON,* didn't have blowholes at the top of their heads for breathing. Like earlier mammals, **THEY HAD NOSTRILS ON TOP OF THEIR NOSES.**

19 *ODOBENOCETOPS,* the walrus whale, was a **SMALL WHALE** with two tusks. In some fossils, one tusk is much longer than the other.

20 Workers building an elementary school on Unalaska Island, in Alaska, U.S.A., found the bones of a new species of **DESMOSTYLIAN.** The manatee-like mammal lived in the sea, but it had four heavy legs with which it paddled about underwater.

21 Seals and sea lions are descended from **BEARLIKE LAND ANIMALS.**

22 Paleobiologist Natalia Rybczynski discovered fossils of a creature she named *PUIJILA DARWINI* in the Arctic. The sleek, three-foot (1-m)-long, 24-million-year-old mammal would have looked like an **OTTER,** but it was an early ancestor of seals.

25 Discovered on the island of Jamaica, *PEZOSIREN* fossils come from a stocky creature with a head like a manatee. The 48-million-year-old mammal, which walked on land and paddled in water, was an early ancestor of manatees and dugongs.

23 Sometimes called an **OTTER-BEAR,** *KOLPONOMOS* was an early seal relative that lived both on land and in the water. With its **POWERFUL JAWS** and downturned snout, it may have scraped mollusks off rocks and crushed them to eat.

24 *LIVYATAN MELVILLEI,* a 12-million-year-old sperm whale, had a toothy 9.8-foot (3-m)-long skull—taller than most ceilings—and could have swallowed a human alive, if any had been around.

1 Museums and research collections around the world hold millions of fossils. **THE BRITISH MUSEUM ALONE HAS SEVEN MILLION.**

2 Museums display fossils for the public, but BEHIND THE SCENES, scientists are studying the specimens as part of their research.

3 MORE THAN 95 PERCENT OF FOSSILS IN MUSEUMS ARE NEVER SHOWN TO THE PUBLIC. Most are stored out of public sight in warehouses and in rooms filled with shelves and drawers.

4 Most museums have at least one **FOSSIL PREPARATION LAB, WHERE FOSSILS ARE CLEANED,** labeled, and prepared for storage. Sometimes those labs are on view so visitors can see the preparators at work.

5

Many universities and state and local parks have great fossil collections. The Yale Peabody Museum of Natural History in New Haven, Connecticut, U.S.A., for instance, contains fossils first collected during the "BONE WARS" BETWEEN OTHNIEL MARSH AND EDWARD DRINKER COPE.

25 MUSEUM

6 **PUTTING TOGETHER A DINOSAUR EXHIBIT INVOLVES MORE THAN JUST SCIENTISTS.** Architects, graphic designers, multimedia specialists, and lighting designers work with the science team to make an exhibit exciting.

7 Big museums have specially trained SCIENTIFIC ILLUSTRATORS ON STAFF. These artists draw specimens for scientific journals and books.

8 SCULPTORS also work in natural history museums to craft models of prehistoric creatures out of FIBERGLASS AND FOAM.

9 **SCIENTISTS AND ARTISTS WORK TOGETHER** to make sure dinosaurs are shown in correct—but fun—positions in museum displays.

10 The fossil hall at the Smithsonian's NATIONAL MUSEUM OF NATURAL HISTORY displays more than 700 prehistoric creatures, including a T. rex.

11 New York City's American Museum of Natural History has several fossil halls, which include a 122-FOOT (37-m) TITANOSAUR and a huge, long-tusked mammoth.

THE TITANOSAUR

12 Chicago's Field Museum is famous for SUE THE T. REX, but it also has MÁXIMO the titanosaur, modeled on a find from Argentina.

13 Pittsburgh's Carnegie Museum of Natural History in the U.S. has MANY ORIGINAL FOSSILS—not models—on display. They include the type specimens for *APATOSAURUS*, *DIPLODOCUS*, and *TYRANNOSAURUS REX*.

14 In Thermopolis, Wyoming, the WYOMING DINOSAUR CENTER has not only dinosaurs from the American West, but also the only *ARCHAEOPTERYX* fossil on display in the United States.

16 THE MUSEUM OF THE ROCKIES in Bozeman, Montana, U.S.A., displays prehistoric mammals and DINOSAURS FROM THE WEST, including Montana's own maiasaurs.

15 In Alberta, Canada, the ROYAL TYRRELL MUSEUM highlights some of Canada's most famous finds, from the Burgess shale's unique creatures to *Albertosaurus* dinosaurs.

18 Originally founded in the 18th century, the NATURAL HISTORY MUSEUM in London, England, has not only dinosaur displays, but also more than 300 scientists on its staff.

17 Berlin, Germany's MUSEUM FÜR NATURKUNDE (Natural History Museum) has the beautiful original *ARCHAEOPTERYX* FOSSIL, as well as many dinosaurs from excavations in Tanzania, Africa.

FACTS ON DISPLAY

19 Dinos from down under are in the NATIONAL DINOSAUR MUSEUM in Canberra, Australia, along with worldwide prehistoric life from 700 million years ago to recent mammals.

20 China is a hotbed for fossil discoveries, and the ZIGONG DINOSAUR MUSEUM in Sichuan Province makes the most of that—it's located right on top of a dinosaur dig.

21 The LA BREA TAR PITS museum in Los Angeles has 3.5 million fossil specimens, including SABER-TOOTHED CATS, giant ground sloths, and one of the world's largest collections of early birds.

25 A 10-year-old boy visiting London's NATURAL HISTORY MUSEUM spotted a MISTAKE IN A DISPLAY. The sign said *Oviraptor* but the picture showed a *PROTOCERATOPS*. After the boy wrote to the museum, the sign was fixed.

22 THE ROYAL ONTARIO MUSEUM in Toronto, Canada, has many original fossil skeletons on display, including Gordo, an 89-foot (27-m)-long *Barosaurus*.

23 The FERNBANK MUSEUM OF NATURAL HISTORY in Atlanta, Georgia, U.S.A., displays fossil casts of some huge Argentinian dinosaurs, including a 123-foot (37-m)-long *Argentinosaurus* (that's twice as long as a tractor trailer).

24 VISIT THE ROYAL BELGIAN INSTITUTE OF NATURAL SCIENCES in Brussels, Belgium, and you'll find a parade of 30 original *IGUANODON* skeletons as well as the original skeleton of "Ben," a 21-foot (6.4-m)-long *PLATEOSAURUS*.

❶ The ancestors of elephants, mastodons, and mammoths evolved in Africa about 50 million years ago.

❷ *Deinotherium giganteum,* an early elephant, was the size of a modern elephant, but it had one very different feature: Its tusks grew out of its bottom jaw and curved downward.

❸ About 19 million years ago, mammoths and mastodons began to migrate to Europe and the Americas.

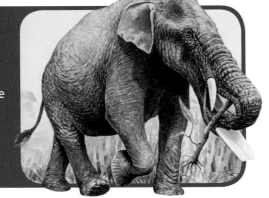

❹ *Amebelodon,* an early elephant from North America, had flattened lower tusks that scooped forward like long shovels. The animal may have used them to dig up plants and scrape bark off trees.

❺ One kind of mastodon, *Mammut borsoni,* had tusks that were longer than the creature was tall. The animal would have had to hold its head up when it walked to keep the tusks from digging into the ground.

❻ Mastodons were shorter than mammoths. They had flatter heads and pointier ridged teeth.

❼ A mastodon tusk found in Greece in 2007 was the largest ever discovered, measuring 16.4 feet (5 m) long.

Mammoths and babies at a watering hole

MAMMOTHS, AND MASTODONS

8 Mammoths could be—mammoth! Based on a leg bone found in Germany, mammoths from the grasslands stood at least 14.8 feet (4.5 m) at the shoulder and weighed up to 15.8 tons (14.3 t), more than twice as heavy as an African elephant.

9 "Zed" the Columbian mammoth, discovered at the **La Brea Tar Pits,** had a rough life. Dying at the old age of 50 or so, he had several broken and healed ribs, as well as arthritis in his joints.

10 The bones of **"Archie" the Columbian mammoth,** now in the University of Nebraska State Museum, were unearthed by chickens pecking at the ground.

11 Fossils found on the Mediterranean island of Cyprus in 1902 came from dwarf elephants about 4.5 feet (1.4 m) tall.

12 Humans and mammoths lived at the same time. Early humans hunted them, painted them on cave walls, and used their skins for tents or beds.

13 A final, lonely colony of mammoths that lived on Russia's Wrangel Island 3,700 years ago had pale, shiny hair.

14 Early hunter-gatherers in Ukraine built huts out of mammoth bones.

15 Some mammoth bodies are so well preserved that scientists can get fragments of DNA—their genetic code—from their cells.

15 BRILLIANT FACTS ABOUT

❶ Fossils can be found not just at remote desert digs, but also in backyards, in local parks, on beaches and riverbanks, and in walls and buildings.

❷ Local fossil hunters learn the geology of their area. They often use geological maps to help them find sedimentary rocks that might hold fossils.

❸ Exposed or eroded sedimentary rocks are the most common places to find fossils. These rocks often have a grainy look, and may have visible layers.

❹ Fossil hunters need to follow safety rules: to go with adults and stay away from roads, construction sites, and private property.

❺ Almost every area has a **fossil or geology group that will help beginners find fossils.**

❻ Polished limestone floors in buildings sometimes contain beautiful fossil specimens.

❼ Stone walls, showing lots of exposed rock faces, can be **good places to search for fossils.**

A tooth fossil of the shark *Carcharodon megalodon* found at Calvert Cliffs State Park, in Maryland, U.S.A.

100

BACKYARD FOSSILS

8 Many fossils are discovered by construction workers. For instance, subway workers in Los Angeles have dug up prehistoric camel, sloth, whale, and mammoth bones.

9 Beach sand often holds ancient **shark teeth.**

10 Most fossils in building stone will be **shells, corals, and other small ocean animals,** which are preserved much more often than animal bones.

11 Even New York City has visible fossils—in its buildings. For instance, **300-million-year-old fossil snails and crinoids** are embedded in the front of Rockefeller Center.

12 Just down from the statue of Lincoln at Washington, D.C.'s Lincoln Memorial, in the cobblestones next to the steps, are burrows of ancient creatures from the **Cambrian period.**

13 Thieves stole headstones from graveyards in Marston Magna, England, after they turned out to be filled with ammonite fossils.

14 One rule for amateurs who find a truly amazing fossil is to not dig it up, but to take a picture and send it to a local paleontology museum for identification.

15 The men's restroom at Washington, D.C.'s National Gallery of Art has **fossil gastropods in its marble walls.**

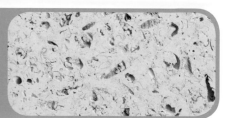

15 UNCHANGED FACTS

1 **Living fossils** are plants and animals that are relatively **unchanged in shape from prehistoric times,** and that have few or no close relatives today.

2 **"Living fossil"** is not a scientific term. All creatures evolve, and no living animals are exactly the same as their prehistoric ancestors.

3 Today's **horseshoe crabs** (which are not crabs, but arthropods related to spiders) closely resemble their Jurassic ancestor, *Mesolimulus*.

4 Sometimes known as **monkey puzzle trees,** araucarias are tall conifers that have existed almost unchanged since the Jurassic period, when sauropods snacked on their branches.

5 **Tiny pelican spiders,** which prey on other spiders, look much like their 50-million-year-old ancestors.

6 **Tuataras, primitive New Zealand reptiles** known as **sphenodontids,** are descended from Mesozoic sphenodontids found in fossils around the world.

7 **The coelacanth, a lobe-finned fish known from 300-million-year-old fossils,** was thought to be long extinct until a South African fisherman caught a live one in 1938.

ABOUT LIVING FOSSILS

8 The rarely seen **frilled shark,** a six-foot (2-m)-long fish with 300 needlelike teeth and named for its frilly-looking gills, is directly descended from similar **Cretaceous sharks.**

9 The leaves of today's *Ginkgo biloba* trees are almost identical to those of fossil ginkgo plants from about 60 million years ago.

10 Some crocodilians—crocodiles, alligators, and gharials—are almost unchanged in shape from 112-million-year-old ancestors such as *Sarcosuchus.*

11 Horsetails, brushy plants that grow from spores rather than seeds, are closely related to ancient horsetails that grew up to 66 feet (20 m) tall about 360 million years ago.

12 Brachiopods known as *Lingula,* which live in narrow shells, have changed very little in shape since their Cambrian ancestors. However, studies show that their genes have evolved quite a bit.

13 The **Australian lungfish can live both in water and on land,** breathing with a single lung. It is similar to 380-million-year-old lungfishes.

14 Many-legged, caterpillar-like velvet worms bear a striking resemblance to ancient Cambrian worm fossils from Canada's Burgess shale.

The biggest known crocodile, which lived two to four million years ago, was 27 feet (8.3 m) long.

15 The duck-billed platypus, an Australian egg-laying mammal, looks much like the Miocene platypus *Obdurodon.*

1 No one knows when life on Earth began. Fossils of microscopic life go back at least 3.5 billion years, but some researchers say they've found evidence of life 3.7 or even 3.9 billion years ago.

2 Scientists aren't sure what caused the Cambrian explosion, when many species suddenly appear in the fossil record. Some think an increase in oxygen in the ocean may have spurred new life.

3 There is ongoing investigation into what killed off 90 percent of all life on Earth at the end of the Permian period, 252 million years ago. Theories include an asteroid hit, volcanic eruptions, and poisonous gases welling up in the ocean.

4 Scientists debate what caused the mass extinction at the end of the Cretaceous period, when all non-bird dinosaurs died out. Evidence exists for an asteroid strike and for massive volcanic eruptions—or perhaps for both at the same time.

5 Just how flying insects evolved is a mystery. The fossil record has a 60-million-year gap between the appearance of the first known insect and the next specimens, which suddenly had wings.

6 It is still unknown how the big pterosaurs launched themselves into the air. Some scientists think they leaped off high places to start. Some believe they ran on two legs before jumping up, while others believe they jumped straight up from four legs.

7 The very first dinosaur is unknown. It might be 228-million-year-old *Eoraptor,* or *Nyasasaurus,* a 243-million-year-old "dinosauriform" from Tanzania—or a creature still undiscovered.

Tsintaosaurus's unicornlike horn may have helped it attract a mate.

PALEONTOLOGY MYSTERIES

8 New fossils keep changing the estimate of the biggest dinosaur. *Argentinosaurus* and *Supersaurus* are contenders, but many size estimates are based just on partial skeletons.

9 Scientists still debate whether dinosaurs were cold-blooded (ectothermic), warm-blooded (endothermic), or somewhere in between (mesothermic). There is evidence for all of these possibilities, though many scientists are leaning toward mesothermic.

10 Why dinosaurs had frills, sails, and crests is unknown. The tall ridges on the backs of dinos like *Spinosaurus* may have helped cool the animals. Or dino decorations may have served as a display, making them noticeable to other dinosaurs.

11 Scientists are unsure whether dinosaurs were **active at night or during the day or both.** Some studies of fossil eye sockets suggest that at least some dinosaurs and pterosaurs traveled by night as well as by day.

12 How the ancestors of birds learned to fly is still being investigated. Did they take off from the ground? Studies of birdlike theropods such as *Microraptor* and *Changyuraptor* may tell us more.

13 Experts aren't sure if all tyrannosaurs had feathers. Some tyrannosaur fossils show a feathery covering, but so far *T. rex* looks simply scaly.

14 Learning how mammals began to fly would be a big discovery. **Bats are the only true flying mammals today,** but we don't know much about how they evolved.

15 It's unknown what (or who) **killed off so many giant mammals** about 10,000 years ago. Some evidence points to **human hunting, but climate change, or other factors,** may also be behind their deaths.

The footprints of a group of early humans, both adults and children, are fossilized in volcanic ash in Tanzania.

 DID YOU KNOW? **ANTHROPOLOGISTS**—scientists who study human beings and their ancestors—**HAVE FOUND MORE THAN 6,000 FOSSIL BONES OF EARLY HUMANS,** and they find more every year.

ANCIENT FOOTPRINTS

About six or seven million years ago, sturdy, apelike primates walked on two legs across the African grass. These human ancestors evolved into many different species as the centuries went by. They began to use stone tools and to cook their food over fires. Starting perhaps 500,000 years ago, early humans began to leave Africa for Europe and the wider world. These pioneers seem to have split into Neanderthals and Denisovans, human species that are now extinct. About 60,000 years ago, possibly earlier, modern humans known as *Homo sapiens* left Africa to join them.

Human fossils tell us much of this story. We still don't know much about the early human species and how they were related. Scientists are still studying and debating the timing of how they migrated from place to place. Even so, a picture is forming of a diverse and adventurous human family.

Bones aren't the only human fossils. We have also found trace fossils in the form of preserved footprints. One famous set of prints, known as the Laetoli footprints, was made by three early humans, possibly the species *Australopithecus afarensis*, who walked through volcanic ash in Laetoli, Tanzania. *Homo sapiens* left behind a more recent set of prints, known as the Engare Sero tracks, on the shores of Lake Natron in Tanzania. Perhaps 19,000 years old, the tracks show us where about a dozen barefoot people, including women and children, trotted and jogged together across the mud, just like a family on an outing today.

GLOSSARY

amphibian a cold-blooded animal that can live in water and on land

angiosperm a flowering plant whose seeds are enclosed within the flower

arachnid a kind of arthropod that has eight legs but no antennae; spiders, scorpions, and ticks are arachnids.

archosaur a member of a group of reptiles that includes dinosaurs, crocodiles, and birds

arthropod a member of a large group of invertebrate animals with segmented bodies and jointed limbs; insects, spiders, and crabs are arthropods.

bacteria (singular: bacterium) single-celled, tiny organisms that live in soil, water, or the bodies of plants and animals

badlands land where few plants grow and the wind and water have worn away the rock into different shapes

blowhole a hole on the top of a whale's head that is used for breathing

bone bed a layer of rock that contains bones—especially one that contains a big collection of bones

brachiopod a mollusk-like sea animal enclosed within two doorlike shells, hinged at the back

bryozoan a small underwater animal that typically lives in connected colonies

ceratopsian a kind of dinosaur, such as *Triceratops*, with horns, a beaky mouth, and a bony frill on its skull

compound eye an eye made of many separate parts, each one of which can detect light

conifer a kind of evergreen tree, usually with needle-shaped leaves

coprolite fossilized animal waste

crest in animals, a ridge sticking up from the head

crinoid a sea animal—a kind of echinoderm—with five or more long arms

crustacean a kind of arthropod, usually living in water, with a tough exoskeleton and two pairs of antennae; crabs and lobsters are crustaceans.

dinosaur a member of a group of extinct plant-eating or meat-eating reptiles that lived in the Mesozoic era

echinoderm a member of a large group of invertebrate sea animals with hard, spiny coverings; sea stars, crinoids, and sea urchins are echinoderms.

echinoid a small sea animal—a kind of echinoderm—that lives on the ocean floor and is enclosed in a thin, rigid covering

echolocation a way of spotting distant objects using reflected sound waves

ectothermic cold-blooded

embryo an unborn animal in the early stages of its development

endothermic warm-blooded

eon the longest span of geologic time, such as the Phanerozoic eon

epoch a geologic time span shorter than a period and longer than an age, such as the Paleocene epoch

Caudipteryx

era a geologic time span shorter than an eon and longer than a period, such as the Mesozoic era

evolution the process by which living things have developed from earlier forms over many generations

evolve to change over time through the process of evolution

exoskeleton the stiff outer covering that supports and protects an animal such as a crab

extinction the process of becoming extinct, to the point that a species no longer has any living members

fossil the preserved remains or traces of an animal or plant that lived in prehistoric times, at least 10,000 years ago

gastrolith a stone that an animal has swallowed to help its digestion

108

Triceratops

genus a group of related plants or animals made up of one or more species

geologic relating to geology, the science of the Earth and its history

hominin a modern human or a modern human's ancestor

index fossil a fossil that belongs to one specific time period and is useful for identifying the age of rocks

invertebrate not having a backbone; animals without backbones are called invertebrates.

keratin a material that makes up hair, fingernails, and hooves

lobe-finned having specialized, muscular fins

microfossil a fossil of a tiny animal or of tiny parts of an animal, best seen through a microscope

nautiloid a sea animal related to the octopus or squid, living inside a curved, straight, or spiral shell

organism a living thing; all plants and animals are organisms.

osteoderm a bony plate in an animal's skin

paleontologist a scientist who studies fossils and the record of ancient life on Earth

paleontology the study of ancient life through fossil remains

period a geologic time span shorter than an era and longer than an epoch, such as the Triassic period

petrified changed into stone

predator an animal that kills and eats other animals

prehistoric from a time before written history

preparator someone who prepares specimens and museum displays

primate a member of the group of mammals that includes humans, apes, and monkeys

radioactive giving off rays and particles as atoms break apart

raptor in paleontology, a dromaeosaur, a small to medium-size predatory dinosaur

reptile a member of a group of cold-blooded, egg-laying, scaly animals such as snakes and lizards

sauropod four-legged, plant-eating saurischian (lizard-hipped) dinosaurs, typically very large with long necks and small heads

scavenger an animal that eats dead or decaying remains of other animals

sediment material, such as sand or soil, that is carried by wind or water before it settles down

sedimentary made from sediment; sedimentary rocks are formed from material that has settled in layers and hardened.

species a group of closely related plants or animals that can breed with one another; species is the scientific classification just below genus.

specimen an item that is collected as a sample to be examined

stromatolite a layered mound or deposit made from both ancient and modern bacteria

synapsid a four-legged land animal that was the ancestor of modern mammals

Trilobite

tetrapod a vertebrate land animal; tetrapods include dinosaurs, amphibians, reptiles, birds, and mammals

therapsid a four-legged land vertebrate descended from synapsids; an ancestor of modern mammals

theropod a two-legged, sharp-clawed, meat-eating dinosaur

type specimen a scientific specimen that is picked to be the best example of its group; also known as holotype

UNESCO an international organization (United Nations Educational, Scientific and Cultural Organization) that promotes peace and helps to protect places with cultural and scientific importance

vertebrae the small bones that make up the backbone

vertebrate having a backbone; animals with backbones are called vertebrates.

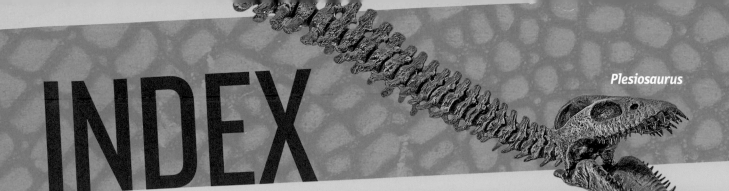

Plesiosaurus

Deinocheirus

Herrerasaurus ischigualastensis

Keichousaurus hui

Pirytized seashell

RESOURCES

To learn more about dinosaurs and fossils, check out these books and websites:

Books

Benton, Mike. *The Kingfisher Dinosaur Encyclopedia.* Macmillan, 2009.

Camper, Cathy. *Bugs Before Time: Prehistoric Insects and Their Relatives.* Simon & Schuster Books for Young Readers, 2002.

Delano, Marfé Ferguson. *Sea Monsters: A Prehistoric Adventure.* National Geographic Kids Books, 2007.

Fern, Tracey. *Barnum's Bones: How Barnum Brown Discovered the Most Famous Dinosaur in the World.* Farrar, Straus and Giroux, 2012.

Gray, Susan. *Paleontology: The Study of Prehistoric Life.* Scholastic, 2012.

Kudlinski, Kathleen. *Boy, Were We Wrong About Dinosaurs!* Puffin, 2008.

Lessem, Don. *Dinosaurs to Dodos: An Encyclopedia of Extinct Animals.* Scholastic, 1999.

Lessem, Don. *Ultimate Dinopedia: The Most Complete Dinosaur Reference Ever,* 2nd ed. National Geographic Kids Books, 2017.

Loxton, Daniel. *Evolution: How We and All Living Things Came to Be.* Kids Can Press, 2010.

Prothero, Donald R., and Mary Persis Williams. *The Princeton Field Guide to Prehistoric Mammals.* Princeton University Press, 2016.

Taylor, Paul D., and Aaron O'Dea. *A History of Life in 100 Fossils.* Smithsonian Books, 2014.

Taylor, Paul D. *Fossil.* Dorling Kindersley, 2017.

Turner, Alan. *National Geographic Prehistoric Mammals.* National Geographic, 2004.

Websites

American Museum of Natural History Paleontology for Kids: amnh.org/explore/ology/paleontology

Brian Switek's Laelaps Blog: blogs.scientificamerican.com/laelaps

Dinosaur National Monument: nps.gov/dino/index.htm

La Brea Tar Pits and Museum: tarpits.org

National Geographic Kids Dinosaurs: kids.nationalgeographic.com/animals/prehistoric-animals

National Geographic Science: nationalgeographic.com/science

National Museum of Natural History Hall of Fossils: naturalhistory.si.edu/exhibits/david-h-koch-hall-fossils-deep-time

Natural History Museum, London, Dino Directory: nhm.ac.uk/discover/dino-directory.html

The Paleontology Portal: paleoportal.org

Sue the *T. Rex*: fieldmuseum.org/blog/sue-t-rex

UC Museum of Paleontology: ucmp.berkeley.edu

CREDITS

AL=Alamy Stock Photo; GI=Getty Images; NGIC=National Geographic Image Collection; SC=Science Source; SS=Shutterstock; ST=Stocktrek Images

Cover: (BACKGROUND), cla78/SS; (UP CTR), Moha El-Jaw/SS; (CTR), Franco Tempesta; (tools), LuFeeTheBear/SS; (CTR RT), Mark Brandon/SS; (LO RT), starmaro/SS; (LO LE), Franco Tempesta; (CTR LE), Lefteris Papaulakis/SS; (ammonite), Yurchyks/SS; (LO CTR), olpo/SS; spine, Ryan M. Bolton/SS; **back cover,** (LE), Millard H. Sharp/SC; (CTR), Akkharat Jarusilawong/SS; (RT), DM7/SS

Interior: 1, DAMNFX/NGIC; 3, Yurchyks/SS; 4-5, Monica Serrano/NGIC; 5 (UP LE), LuFeeTheBear/SS; 5 (UP RT), Moha El-Jaw/SS; 5 (LO RT), Akkharat Jarusilawong/SS; 5 (LO LE), Elenarts/SS; 6, Franco Tempesta; 7, AuntSpray/SS; 8-9 (BACKGROUND), Robert Clark/NGIC; 8 (2), Jonathan Blair/NGIC; 8 (3), NASA; 8 (4), tinkivinki/SS; 8 (5), Science History Images/AL; 9 (6), Franco Tempesta; 9 (9), Kenneth Garrett/NGIC; 9 (10), Franco Tempesta; 10 (UP LE), AuntSpray/SS; 10 (UP CTR), Franco Tempesta; 10 (UP RT), Michael Rosskothen/SS; 10 (LO RT), Dorling Kindersley ltd/AL; 10 (LO CTR), Tom & Therisa Stack/Tom Stack & Associates; 10 (LO LE), Paul Fleet/SS; 11 (UP LE), Franco Tempesta; 11 (UP CTR), Franco Tempesta; 11 (UP RT), anibal/Adobe Stock11 (LO RT), Franco Tempesta; 11 (LO CTR), Filipao Photography/SS; 11 (LO LE), Franco Tempesta; 12-13, NG Maps; 12 (UP), Warpaint/SS; 12 (CTR), Scott Camazine/AL; 12 (LO), Warpaint/SS; 13 (UP), Catmando/SS; 13 (LO), DM7/SS; 14-15, George F. Mobley/NGIC; 16-17, Sidney Hastings/NGIC; 16 (UP RT), kamnuan/SS; 16 (3), NASA/Robert Markowitz; 16 (5), Ariantolog/SS; 16 (7), Sabena Jane Blackbird/AL; 17 (8), garanga/SS; 17 (10), arousa/SS; 17 (14), Marco Ansaloni/SC; 18-19, Auscape/UIG/REX/SS; 18 (1), Natursports/SS; 18 (5), Universal Images Group North America LLC/DeAgostini/AL; 18 (7), Kam Mak/NGIC; 19 (8), Sabena Jane Blackbird/AL; 19 (10), O. Louis Mazzatenta/NGIC; 19 (12), O. Louis Mazzatenta/NGIC; 19 (14), Kam Mak/NGIC; 20-21, Marvin Mattelson/NGIC; 22-23, bcampbell65/SS; 22 (8), wacpan/SS; 22 (10), Miguel G. Saavedra/SS; 22 (15), Arpad Benedek/GI; 22 (18), Dorling Kindersley Ltd/AL; 23 (24), Dinoton/SS; 23 (28), Elena Schweitzer/SS; 23 (39), Warpaint/SS; 23 (43), Breck P. Kent/SS; 24-25, Merlin74/SS; 26 (1), Sergii Figurnyi/SS; 26 (2), Warpaint/SS; 26 (3), Sabena Jane Blackbird/AL; 26 (9), Eric Isselee/SS; 26 (10), Dotted Yeti/SS; 27 (13), DeAgostini/GI; 27 (16), National Park Service; 27 (17), Heritage Auctions/REX/SS; 27 (19), Science History Images/AL; 27 (21), Warpaint/SS; 27 (23), O. Louis Mazzatenta/NGIC; 27 (24), Mark_Kostich/SS; 28-29, Raul Martin/NGIC; 28 (1), fivespots/SS; 28 (3), Jonathan Blair/NGIC; 28 (5), Dani Vincek/SS; 28 (7), Linda Bucklin/SS; 29 (8), Charles R. Knight/NGIC; 29 (10), Walter Myers/ST/NGIC; 29 (13), The Natural History Museum/AL; 30-31, Franco Tempesta; 32 (2), Franco Tempesta; 32 (3), Historia/REX/SS; 32 (6), Layne Kennedy/Dembinsky Photo Associates/AL; 32 (9), Artens/SS; 32 (10), Franco Tempesta; 33 (13), Breck P. Kent/SS; 33 (16), David Dilcher; 33 (17), Cultura/M. Suchea and I.V. Tudose/GI; 33 (18), Paul A. Zahl/NGIC; 33 (20), George Poinar; 33 (22), Anastasiia Skorobogatova/SS; 33 (23), National Park Service; 33 (25), National Park Service; 34-35, Paul A. Zahl/NGIC; 36 (1), Franco Tempesta; 36 (3), Franco Tempesta; 36 (4), The Picture Art Collection/AL; 36 (6), ST/NGIC; 36 (7), Franco Tempesta; 36 (9), ST/NGIC; 36 (11), ST/NGIC; 37 (12), ST/NGIC; 37 (13), Lucasfilm/Sunset Boulevard/Corbis via GI; 37 (15), Andrew Francis Wallace/Toronto Star via GI; 37 (17), Subbotina Anna/SS; 37 (19), Erika Kirkpatrick/SS; 37 (24), IBL/REX/SS; 38-39, paleontologist natural/SS; 40-41, Warpaint/SS; 40 (3), The History Collection/AL; 40 (5), Jonathan Blair/NGIC; 40 (6), Art work by Stephen Roberts/DeAgostini/GI; 40 (7), ST/NGIC; 41 (UP), Raul Martin/NGIC; 41 (9), Michael Rosskothe/SS; 41 (12), Akkharat Jarusilawong/SS; 41 (15), ST/NGIC; 42 (1), Damnfx/NGIC; 42 (2), Dotted Yeti/SS; 42 (3), Li Chun; 42 (6), Michael Rosskothen/SS; 42 (10), Robert F. Sisson/NGIC; 42 (11), Richard T. Nowitz/SC; 42 (12), nattanan726/SS; 43 (14), Sementer/SS; 43 (15), Tom Wang/Dreamstime; 43 (16), Neil Lockhart/SS; 43 (19), The Natural History Museum/AL; 43 (20), Roger Harris/SC; 43 (23), ST/NGIC; 44 (3), imageBROKER/REX/SS; 44 (5), Linnas/SS; 44 (6), Petr Tkachev/SS; 44 (8), Natural Visions/AL; 44 (9), The Natural History Museum/AL; 44 (10), Catmando/SS; 45 (12), The Natural History Museum/AL; 45 (14), Warpaint/SS; 45 (15), Jonathan Blair/NGIC; 45 (19), Jonathan Blair/NGIC; 45 (20), Sven Tränkner, Senckenberg; 45 (21), Michael Probst/AP/REX/SS; 45 (22), Gerald Mayr, Seckenberg; 45 (23), AuntSpray/SS; 46-47 (ALL), Franco Tempesta; 48-49, Franco Tempesta; 48 (1), ST/NGIC; 48 (3), National Geographic/NGIC; 48 (5), ST/NGIC; 48 (9), Franco Tempesta; 49 (9), ST/NGIC; 49 (10), ST/NGIC; 49 (13), Valentyna Chukhlyebova/SS; 49 (15), ST/NGIC; 50-51, Catmando/SS; 52-53, Franco Tempesta; 52 (UP), Warpaint/SS; 52 (4), sunsinger/SS; 52 (5), Millard H. Sharp/SC; 52 (7), ST/NGIC; 53 (8), Herschel Hoffmeyer/SS; 53 (10), Universal Images Group North America LLC/DeAgostini/AL; 53 (12), Elenarts/SS; 53 (14), Franco Tempesta; 54-55, Elenarts/SS; 56-57, Franco Tempesta; 56 (1), Franco Tempesta; 56 (5), Sabena Jane Blackbird/AL; 56 (7), EmeCeDesigns/SS; 57 (10), Catmando/SS; 57 (12), Millard H. Sharp/SC; 57 (13), ST/NGIC; 58 (4), Franco Tempesta; 58 (5), Franco Tempesta; 58 (6), Catmando/SS; 58 (7), Franco Tempesta; 58 (9), Herschel Hoffmeyer/SS; 58 (10), ColoArt/SS; 58 (11), Marques/SS; 59 (16), Reimar/SS; 59 (17), Franco Tempesta; 59 (20), Franco Tempesta; 59 (22), Franco Tempesta; 59 (23), Education Images/UIG via GI; 60-61, Franco Tempesta; 60 (2), Nikreates/AL; 60 (5), Franco Tempesta; 60 (7), The Natural History Museum/AL; 61 (8), History and Art Collection/AL; 61 (13), Franco Tempesta; 61 (15), Franco Tempesta; 62-63, Pol O Gradaigh/picture-alliance/dpa/AP Images; 62 (1), Maria Stenzel/NGIC; 62 (3), Roger Tidman/FLPA/imageBROKER/REX/SS; 62 (4), Robin Siegel/NGIC; 63 (8), Isaiah Nengo/NGIC; 63 (10), Lynn Johnson/NGIC; 63 (12), Gautier22/SS; 64 (2), Herschel Hoffmeyer/SS; 64 (3), Catmando/SS; 64 (6), Michael Rosskothen/SS; 64 (7), Franco Tempesta; 64 (8), Michael Rosskothen/SS; 64 (9), Catmando/SS; 65 (14), Darla Zelenitsky; 65 (15), Sinibomb Images/AL; 65 (16), Roman Uchytel; 65 (18), Roman Uchytel; 65 (21), Warpaint/SS; 66-67, O. Louis Mazzatenta/NGIC; 66 (3), CookiesForDevo/SS; 66 (5), Sergey Krasovskiy/GI/ST; 66 (10), Franco Tempesta; 67 (24), Michael Rosskothen/SS; 67 (43), Crudelitas/SS; 68 (1), Michael Skrepnick/NGIC; 68 (3), Marques/SS; 68 (4), Catmando/SS; 68 (6), DM7/SS; 68 (7), DM7/SS; 68 (11), AP Photo/The Billings Gazette, Michael Milstein; 69 (13), Franco Tempesta; 69 (17), Catmando/SS; 69 (CTR), Jean-Michel Girar/SS; 69 (18), Franco Tempesta; 69 (20), AP Photo/Reed Saxon; 69 (21), ST/NGIC; 69 (22), Brian Engh; 70-71, Herschel Hoffmeyer/SS; 72-73, Franco Tempesta; 72 (3), Franco Tempesta; 72 (6), Millard H. Sharp/SC; 72 (7), Franco Tempesta; 73 (8), The Natural History Museum/AL; 73 (11), Prisma Archivo/AL; 73 (12), Linda Bucklin/SS; 74-75, Franco Tempesta; 74 (1), Franco Tempesta; 74 (3), Franco Tempesta; 74 (5), Warpaint/SS; 75 (UP), Valentyna Chukhlyebova/SS; 75 (8), Franco Tempesta; 75 (12), Franco Tempesta; 75 (14), Franco Tempesta; 76-77, Herschel Hoffmeyer/SS; 76 (1), Ryan M. Bolton/SS; 76 (3), Franco Tempesta; 76 (4), The Natural History Museum, London/SC; 76 (6), Nico Ott/SS; 77 (8), Warpaint/SS; 77 (12), Warpaint/SS; 77 (14), guentermanaus/SS; 78-79, Dimitri Carol/AL; 78 (1), Catmando/SS; 78 (3), David Clark/Dinosaurs Alive/Giant Screen Films; 78 (5), O. Louis Mazzatenta/NGIC; 79 (12), O. Louis Mazzatenta/NGIC; 79 (14), Warpaint/SS; 79 (15), Lanmas/AL; 80-81, NPS Photo/Jake Holgerson; 82 (3), Franco Tempesta; 82 (4), Petr Tkachev/SS; 82 (5), Franco Tempesta; 82 (6), Dariush M/SS; 82 (7), Julius T. Csotonyi/SC; 82 (8), Robert Clark/NGIC; 82 (9), Franco Tempesta; 82 (11), Ryan McKellar/Royal Saskatchewan Museum; 83 (14), John Sibbick/NGIC; 83 (16), John Cancalosi/Photolibrary/GI; 83 (17), kzww/SS; 83 (24), Franco Tempesta; 84-85, Jim Zuckerman/GI; 84 (1), Franco Tempesta; 84 (4), Franco Tempesta; 84 (6), Library Book Collection/AL; 85 (9), Christian Musat/SS; 85 (11), Herschel Hoffmeyer/SS; 85 (14), ST/NGIC; 86-87, O. Louis Mazzatenta/NGIC; 86 (1), Franco Tempesta; 86 (2), Imaginechina via AP Images; 86 (7), Franco Tempesta; 87 (8), Catmando/SS; 87 (10), Elenarts/SS; 87 (12), Velizar Simeonovski/Field Museum of Natural History; 88-89, Christian Jegou/Publiphoto/SC; 88 (UP), Catmando/SS; 88 (2), gorosan/SS; 88 (3), ArtCookStudio/SS; 88 (7), Courtesy of Diane Scott; 89 (8), The Natural History Museum, London/SC; 89 (11), Tim Boyle/GI; 89 (14), John Sibbick/NGIC; 90-91, Franco Tempesta; 92-93, Michael Nichols/NGIC; 92 (3), Mauricio Anton/NGIC; 92 (4), miha de/SS; 92 (14), Franco Tempesta; 93 (24), Charles R. Knight/NGIC; 93 (37), Mark Hallett/NGIC; 93 (41), Franco Tempesta; 94 (3), Wlad74/SS; 94 (4), The Natural History Museum/AL; 94 (7), Yann-Hubert/GI/iStockphotos; 94 (9), Nobumichi Tamura; 94 (10), Victor Boswell/NGIC; 94 (12), Holger Kirk/SS; 95 (13), Roman Uchytel; 95 (16), ST/NGIC; 95 (18), Angelique clic/SS; 95 (22), Roman Uchytel; 95 (23), Roman Uchytel; 96 (1), Mykolastock/SS; 96 (4), George Mobley/NGIC; 96 (5), Historic Collection/AL;96 (6), Leon Neal/AFP/GI; 96 (8), Kurt F. Mutchler/NGIC; 96 (11), Justin Lane/Epa/REX/SS; 97 (13), AP Photo/Andrew Rush; 97 (15), Nick Fox/SS; 97 (16), Danita Delimont/AL; 97 (21), Martin Shields/AL; 97 (23), Richard Nowitz/NGIC; 98-99, Raul Martin/NGIC; 98 (2), Catmando/SS; 98 (4), Universal Images Group North America LLC/DeAgostini/AL; 98 (6), Raul Martin/NGIC; 99 (10), Valentina_S/SS; 99 (12), Peter V. Bianchi/NGIC; 99 (14), Sisse Brimberg/NGIC; 100-101, Maria M. Mudd/NGIC; 100 (1), National Park Service; 100 (3), National Park Service; 100 (5), All Canada Photos/AL; 101 (11), JJFarquitectos/GI/iStock; 101 (13), Sabena Jane Blackbird/AL; 101 (15), Philip Openshaw/GI/iStockphoto; 102-103, Franco Tempesta; 102 (1), Mark Thiessen/NGIC; 102 (5), Piotr Naskrecki/Minden Pictures/NGIC; 102 (7), Corey A. Ford/Dreamstime; 103 (8), Kelvin Aitken/VWPics via AP Images; 103 (12), Suphatthra olovedog/SS; 103 (14), O. Louis Mazzatenta/NGIC; 104-105, Franco Tempesta; 104 (1), Alan Uster/SS; 104 (3), Esteban De Armas/SS; 104 (5), O. Louis Mazzatenta/NGIC; 105 (8), Franco Tempesta;105 (12), John Sibbick/NGIC; 105 (14), Farinoza/Dreamstime; 106-107, Robert Clark/NGIC; 108 (UP), Moha El-Jaw/SS; 108 (tools), LuFeeTheBear/SS; 108 (LO), Catmando/SS; 109 (UP), starmaro/SS; 109 (LO), Dinoton/SS; 110 (UP), Lefteris Papaulakis/SS; 110 (LO), Linda Bucklin/SS; 111 (UP LE), Millard H. Sharp/SC; 111 (UP CTR), Mark Brandon/SS; 111 (brush), LuFeeTheBear/SS; 111 (LO), Yurchyks/SS

Since 1888, the National Geographic Society has funded more than 12,000 research, exploration, and preservation projects around the world. The Society receives funds from National Geographic Partners, LLC, funded in part by your purchase. A portion of the proceeds from this book supports this vital work. To learn more, visit natgeo.com/info.

NATIONAL GEOGRAPHIC and Yellow Border Design are trademarks of the National Geographic Society, used under license.

For more information, visit nationalgeographic.com,
call 1-877-873-6846, or write to the following address:

National Geographic Partners
1145 17th Street N.W.
Washington, D.C. 20036-4688 U.S.A.

Visit us online at nationalgeographic.com/books

For librarians and teachers:
nationalgeographic.com/books/librarians-and-educators/

More for kids from National Geographic: natgeokids.com

National Geographic Kids magazine inspires children to explore their world with fun yet educational articles on animals, science, nature, and more. Using fresh storytelling and amazing photography, *Nat Geo Kids* shows kids ages 6 to 14 the fascinating truth about the world—and why they should care. **kids.nationalgeographic.com/subscribe**

For information about special discounts for bulk purchases,
please contact National Geographic Books Special Sales:
specialsales@natgeo.com

For rights or permissions inquiries, please contact National Geographic Books Subsidiary Rights: bookrights@natgeo.com

Designed by Christopher L. Mazzatenta

National Geographic supports K–12 educators with ELA Common Core Resources. Visit natgeoed.org/commoncore for more information.

Library of Congress Cataloging-in-Publication Data

Names: Daniels, Patricia, 1955- author.
Title: 1,000 facts about dinosaurs, fossils, and prehistoric life / Patricia Daniels.
Other titles: One thousand facts about dinosaurs, fossils, and prehistoric life
Description: Washington : National Geographic Kids, 2020. | Series: 1,000 facts about | Includes index. | Audience: Ages 8-12 | Audience: Grades 4-6 | Summary: "From dinosaurs like Stegosaurus and Giganotosaurus that ruled the land to the mammoths and giant sloths that followed them, discover all you have ever wanted to know about dinosaurs, fossils, and prehistoric life. Uncover amazing fossil facts about the first four-legged creatures; find out what it's like to be on a dinosaur dig; and marvel at some of the fiercest, most fascinating claws and teeth. Learn how dinosaurs and birds are connected, find out the biggest prehistoric mysteries that scientists are still trying to crack, and sink your teeth into some seriously supersize dino stats"-- Provided by publisher.
Identifiers: LCCN 2019034673 | ISBN 9781426336676 (hardcover) | ISBN 9781426336683 (library binding)
Subjects: LCSH: Paleontology--Juvenile literature. | Dinosaurs--Juvenile literature. | Fossils--Juvenile literature.
Classification: LCC QE714.5 .D26 2020 | DDC 567.9--dc23
LC record available at https://lccn.loc.gov/2019034673

The publisher would like to thank everyone who worked to make this book possible. From Potomac Global Media: Kevin Mulroy, Barbara Brownell Grogan, Christopher L. Mazzatenta, Margaret Sidlosky, Patricia Daniels, Matthew Vrazo, Heather McElwain, and Timothy Griffin. From National Geographic: Angela Modany, associate editor; Brett Challos, art director; Sarah J. Mock, senior photo editor; Mike McNey, map production; Sean Philpotts, production director; Sally Abbey, managing editor; Molly Reid, production editor; and Anne LeongSon and Gus Tello, design production assistants.

Printed in China
19/RRDH/1